*In memory of Karpov.*

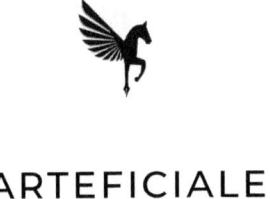

# ARTEFICIALE

Curated by Matteo Carria.

# TABLE OF CONTENTS

# PREFACE

Maria Giacomello, also known as Karpov, was a painter of the 20th century, variously defined by critics as neorealist, surrealist, and futurist. During her artistic period, the moods of the time, as well as her most remote thoughts, became essential material for composing numerous authentic poems, revealing an intimate and irresistible drive to express herself through art. The poems gathered in this book, accompanied by some photos of Karpov's paintings, represent only a small portion of the artist's archive.

However, Karpov is not the only protagonist of this story: within the images of this book, a second artist hides. It is an enigmatic opponent with unpredictable abilities, who challenges the artist to a competition of emotional expression: it is artificial intelligence.

Each poem in this book is matched with an image whose source will not be declare, with the purpose of arousing perplexity in the reader. Some of these pictures are photographs of the artist's original paintings, while others are digital images generated by an artificial intelligence algorithm according to technical parameters and stylistic suggestions. The following author's file, with its detailed description of Karpov's artistic style, can be helpful in identifying some significant differences.

In the field of artificial intelligence, there are algorithms capable of generating astonishing images. They start from a wide database of available information and they operate according to textual requests. For instance, if I want to generate an impressionist painting of a galloping horse, I just have to type it: in the span of few seconds the algorithm will deliver an image faithful to my request, following statistical parameters. All of this is made possible by the initial data, the way they are sorted, the level of detail in my request, and the computing power.

It can be considered a proper revolution in the generation of images. The one who writes the prompt - the textual request - can be considered the author. The more complete the text (with information, parameters, and stylistic choices) the more the algorithm will be stimulated to generate something original, fulfilling the request. And since images generated by algorithms are claiming prizes in some art competitions - see Jason Allen's work "Théâtre D'opéra Spatial" - we can affirm that artificial intelligence is actually capable of creating true works of art.

Finally, this book itself is further evidence of the power of art to make us reflect on ourselves and the world around us. It is an invitation to look beyond the mere excitement of using new technologies. Rather, it wants to elicit questions about our relationship with machines and the immense responsibility they deliver to us. Thus, an existential challenge is presented, one that cannot leave us untouched: if artistic value can be defined independently from the instrument, and consequently even an algorithm can create works of art, then what does the term "art" refer to today?

# KARPOV

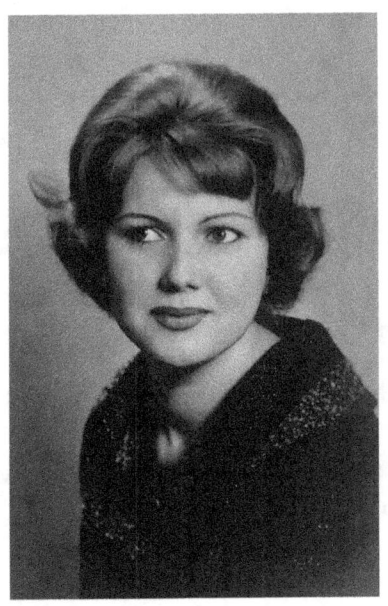

Maria Giacomello
*Bucarest, 1935 - Vigevano, 2019*

*Surrealism in the image, impressionism in color,*
*a pictorial whirlwind that becomes substance.*

Karpov. An original pseudonym, chosen to sign her work in remembrance of her Eastern European origins. A vibrant and versatile painter who conveys sensations stemming from her restless, extroverted, passionate, and impetuous-till-rebellion soul. A whirlwind of signs, shapes, and colors that envelop everything and lead back to an artistic journey suddenly bloomed at the age of six and evolved over six decades filled with study, research, and dedication. Karpov's whole artistic life was nothing but a long creative period that witnessed the professional metamorphosis of the artist, afterwards variously defined by critics as neorealist, surrealist, and futurist.

Defining her style is challenging because her work, in different phases of evolution, tends to always reflect that emotional vortex that flows like lava from the interior of a crater unable to contain its essence. What elicits emotions in those who admire Karpov's art is her special ability to connect with the inner world of the observer, seeking a dialogue with their most subconscious instincts. Her work reveals a firm rejection of formalisms, beliefs, and subjection to the forms and styles of others. In fact, the fundamental traits and lines of her paintings are devoid of preconceived and academic calculation, despite the many years of professional training and the artist's perfectionism, first in Romania and then in Italy.

Thus, the interpretive key to Karpov's work escapes the norms, which the artist seems to deliberately overlook, to achieve full freedom and improvisation for her creative drive. The chromatic effects of ochre, reds, and yellows that illuminate the skies reveal new, unlimited spaces to the observer's imagination. Games of color and lines merge into expressions and visions projected beyond time and space, in a dimension that, even if subjective, still remains accessible to the attentive and sensitive observer. Karpov's painting is characterized by decisive brushwork, without second thoughts: she loves to express herself through the essential nature of the stroke, sometimes soft and harmonious, sometimes strong and vibrant.

The artist's inner tension appears in the controlled and coordinated whirlwinds that animate the creative vortex of her compositions, bringing to light her own intimate restlessness, that surreal and metaphysical anxiety only proper to her. The emblematic concentric circles that fade away into the infinite are to be understood as symbols of the artist's dynamic opposition to the anxieties of life itself and the daily struggle to rise and not just survive.

From this emotional universe, Karpov releases her spirit, brimming with vitality, but also with rebellion against stasis, with an impulse to escape from the oppressive cage of the often-contained and regulated life of modern humanity. The artist rather lives and acts based on her intimate and irresistible urge to manifest herself through art, in the whirlwind of her effects and the explosion of colors, in a natural and impulsive style, devoid of calculation, true. A critic once said that Karpov's painting is permeated with poetry and suggestive harmonies, almost "a yearning for universal brotherhood".

Her relentless quest to merge different worlds of sensitivity and culture shines through the dreamy and romantic atmospheres of her paintings. Contemplating them, the viewer is captivated by pastel colors tending to transfigure plastic visions, figures, dance movements, and even certain popular landscapes of her native land, the distant and unforgettable Romania.

Recalled images with depictions of Moldavian folk scenes, true holograms of the past. Some works appear to be influenced by the evolution of post-war Romanian art. But perhaps, the artist's intention is precisely to seek a dialogue with those who can visually and intimately filter her work in a personal and interpretive way. Everything is as if Karpov wanted to gently unveil her own secrets to the observer, searching for a deeper and dreamlike form of communication. The instinctive visions and symbolic figures in her works express the desire to bring together historical memory and the reality of the present. Two parallel worlds that seem to coexist sculpted in her paintings, in an endless, liberating research.

# POEMS

*" For now, no words and no comments:*
*time will bestow its mature fruit*
*on art, and on my poetry which is cry. "*

## Sailing among the stars

The umbilical cord
was torn away
and for a day
you were my creature.

I saw you passing and passing again...
I've been standing still for centuries,
between the Sun and Earth,
between the Moon and Mars.

I see you carrying messages
of love to the Moon,
like a meteor, I make
a trail of fire to hit you.

And there, finally,
I thought you would stay.
I yearn for, feeling your heart
beating for everyone,
looking up, I sweated,
I sweated cold for you.

I suddenly pitied myself
and desired light, joy, life,
to fly, navigate that unconscious,
hidden, intimate hope
that instinctively made me blow you,
and you... entered the corridor of life.

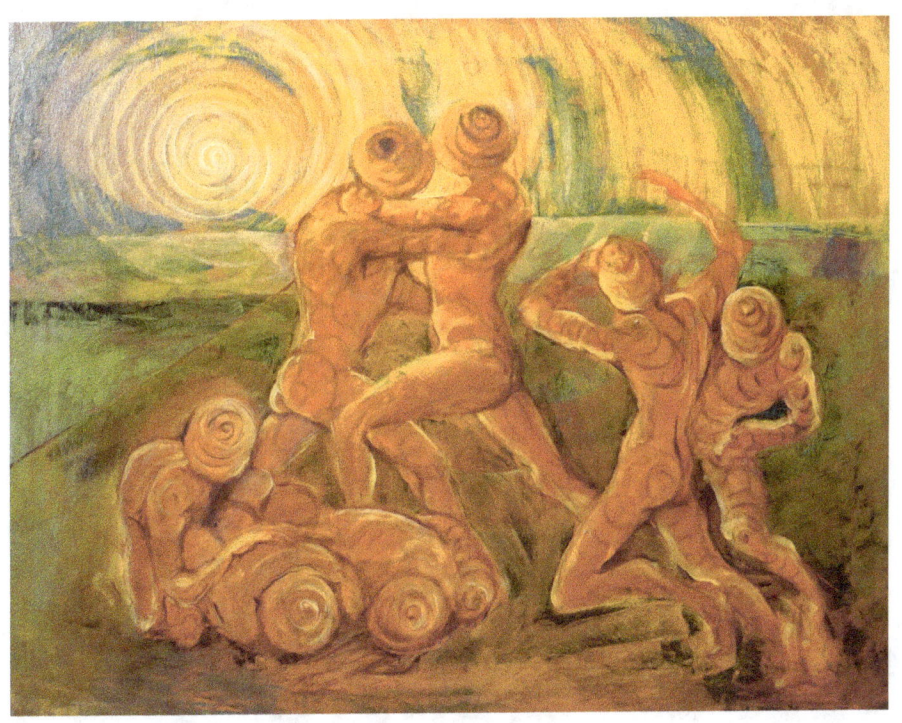

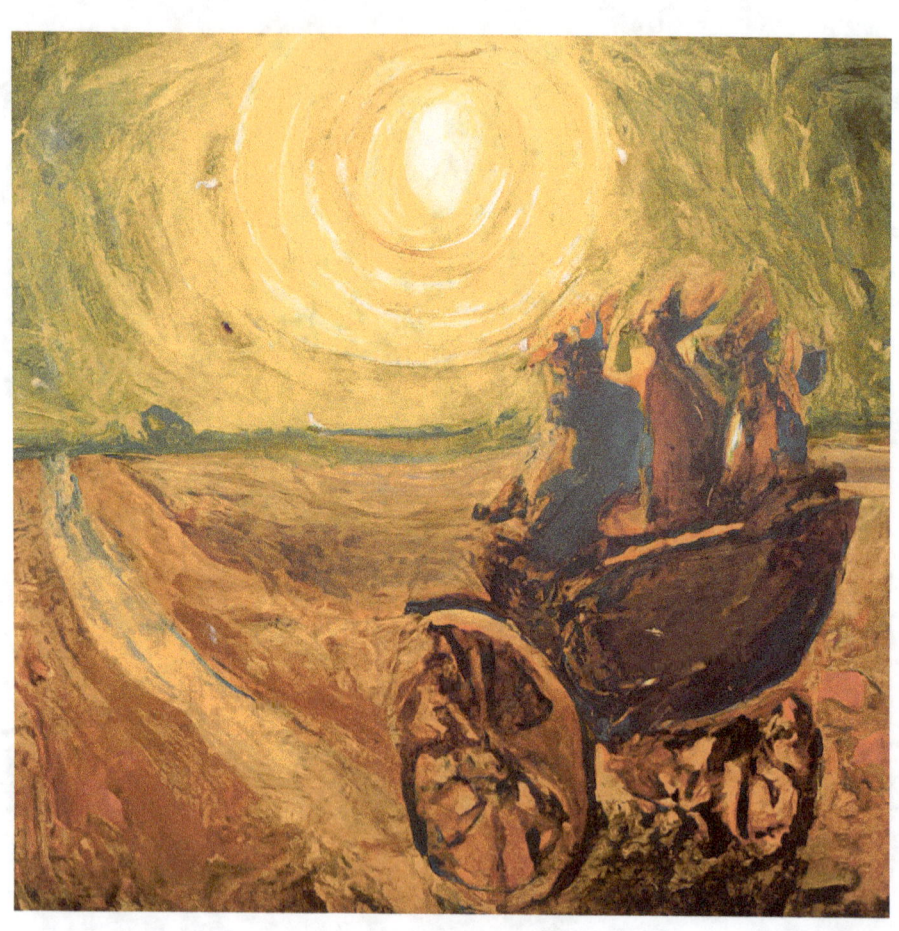

# Ranting

*The truth is open*
*open upwards,*
*as creation is unfolded.*

*The superhuman made*
*revealed to us, and many are*
*the counting means.*

*A dual movement*
*exists even in the stars*
*on every planet and everywhere,*
*even in us, the code lies*
*dreamlike binary, genetic lived.*

*Not alien uniform*
*and virginal archetypes, but*
*multiple cosmic beings.*
*Word, truth, and life from father*
*to son, from mother to daughter.*

*Love projects itself,*
*perceives itself, feels itself.*

*It knows it belongs to the universe*
*and is ignited by being wise.*

## Wrongly denied

*They tied him up,
they gagged him,
they accused him,
and they took everything from him,
bread, clothing, ideas,
the breath and the voice,
"You don't deserve us,"
they shouted.*

*Throwing him into the pit
of forced labor.
Death called:
he witnessed her,
swore to have loved her,
and she saved him.*

## Sins

*Thieving men
with jewel cases
of joys and preciouses,
all to defend.*

*Little corrupted
repentant beings.*

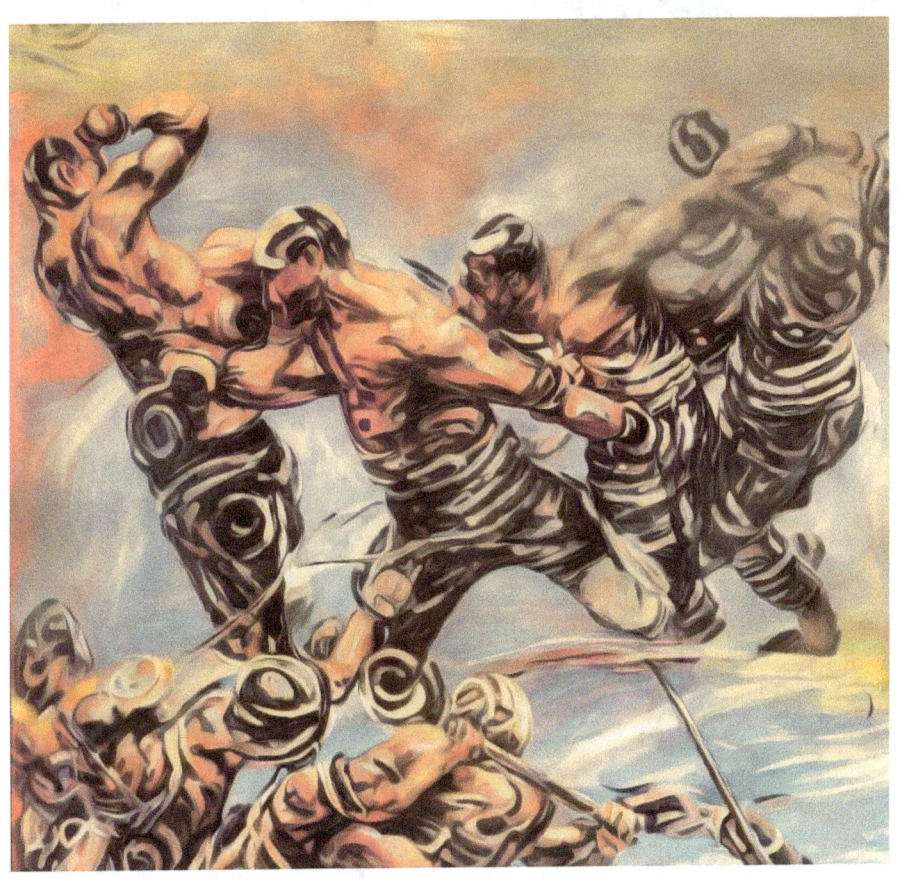

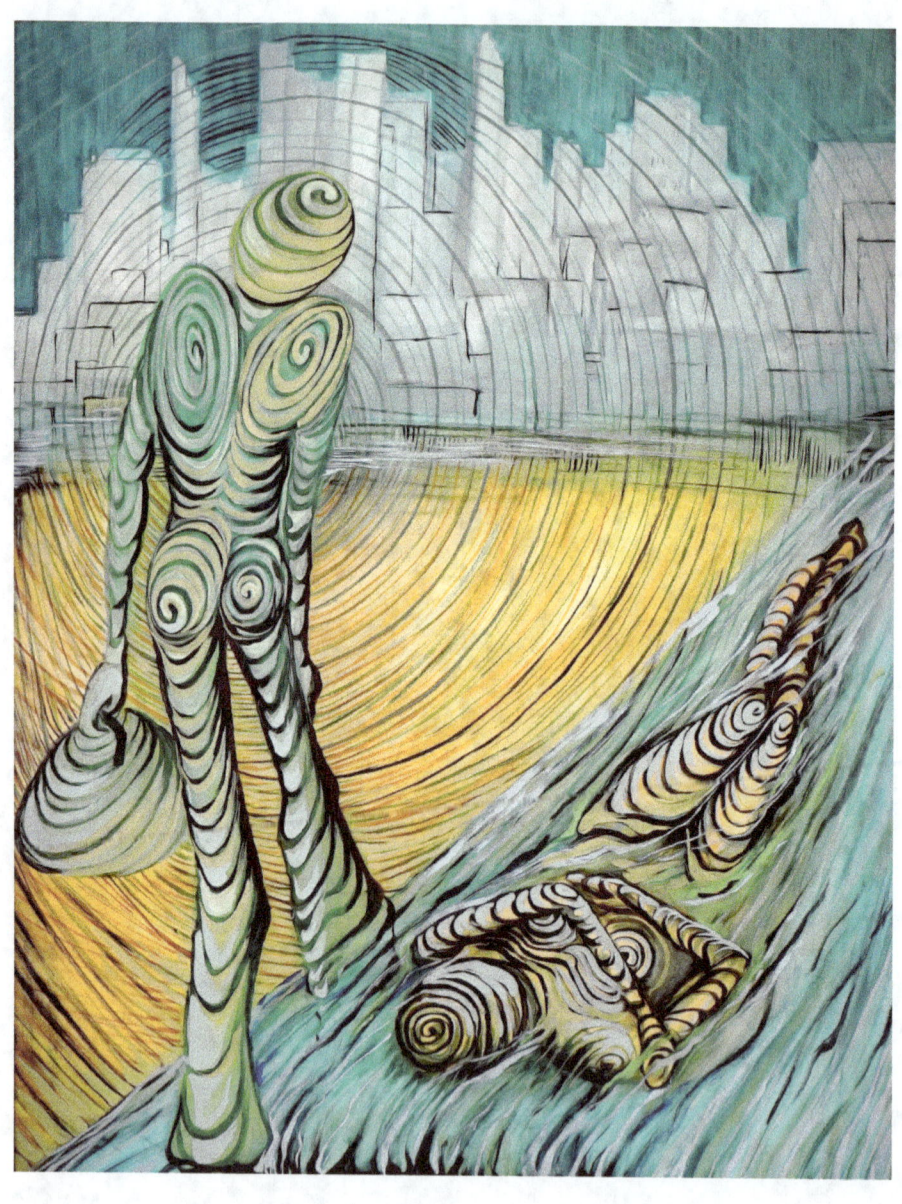

# The robot partisan

*Sheltered from the sun,*
*the robot partisan,*
*under the blossoming sunflower plants*
*of Bassarabia.*

*Lying at their roots,*
*amazed he admires the blue sky,*
*the infinite background*
*of these yellow sunflower heads.*

*Hours dance around you,*
*for you that wait the night,*
*and slowly, slowly move.*
*Slow clouds contrast with thoughts,*
*that slip, white...*
*And now the sun winks again.*

*The heads bow,*
*yellow, under a breath of wind,*
*warm, scented with grass*
*and sunflower, burnt, scorched.*
*The hours dance around again,*
*and slowly, slowly you turn your head.*

*The sun sets,*
*and the futile effort quiets down,*
*and quiets down the trouble,*
*calming the mind and heart.*
*The night descends,*
*the accomplice of the sunflower's robot partisan.*

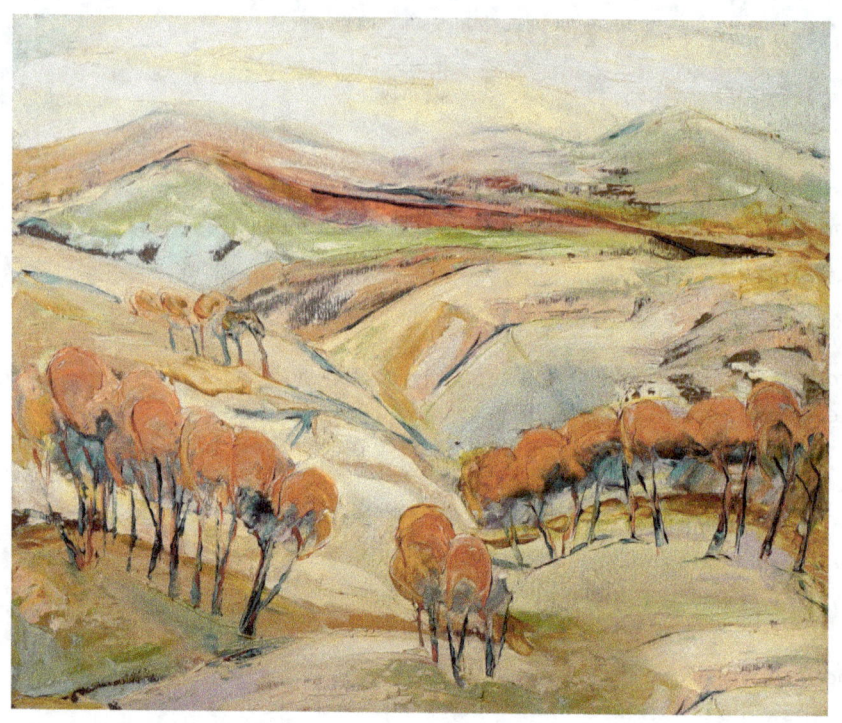

## Ring around

*I play ring-around,*
*... let the world fall,*
*... the earth,*
*to get lost with you,*
*to feel my head spin,*
*to see the immense sky,*
*to feel childish again,*
*to feel close to you.*

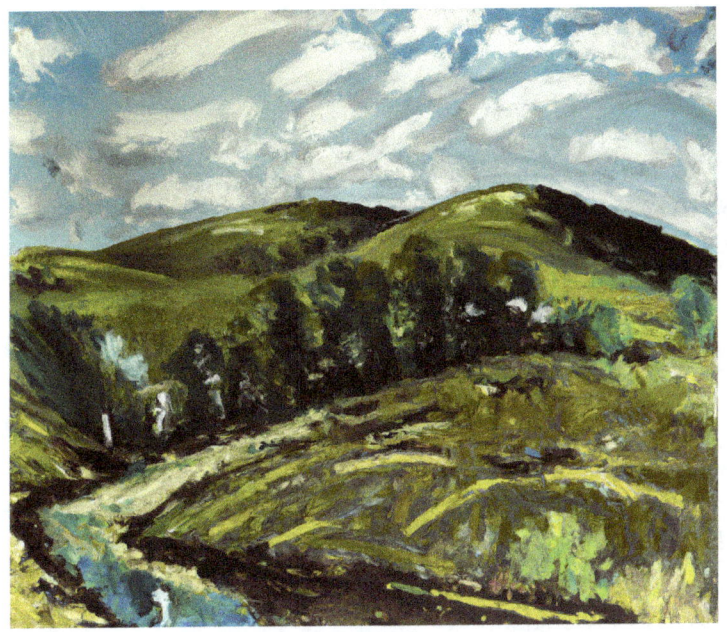

## Letter

The wind darts.
Clothes are hanged between the legs.
Swallows and dry leaves
chase each other.

Amid the agony
of wet tree branches,
I still search incredulously,
at the bottom of my pockets,
for that garden of thoughts
that was your letter.

## Respite

The little red flag was enough,
was enough the salt in the air
to squeeze my heart,
even the wind wanted to push,
toward the trace of your memory.

Wave the farewell little flag
to the sea that swells.

I feel the breathlessness of the water
wanting to swallow my brain.

I review and land in memory,
in the waves, I saw you adrift.
The rain followed you,
and gave me respite, slipping away
in search of you.


## Ideal

In pitch darkness, I can't see you.
But I sense you on my skin,
in my heart.

I deeply feel,
sense your presence,
you are embodied in me.

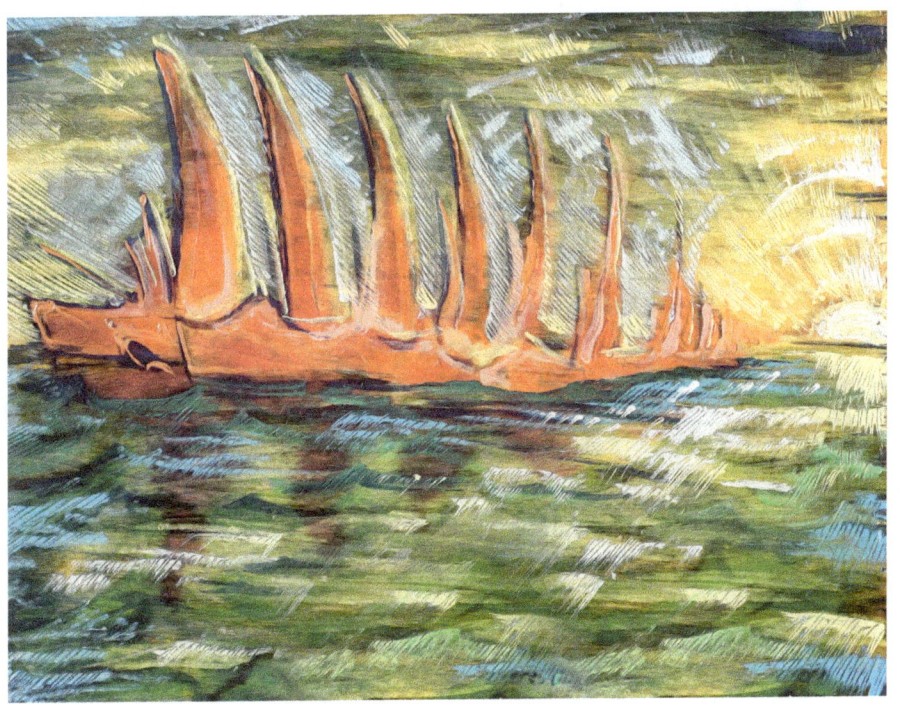

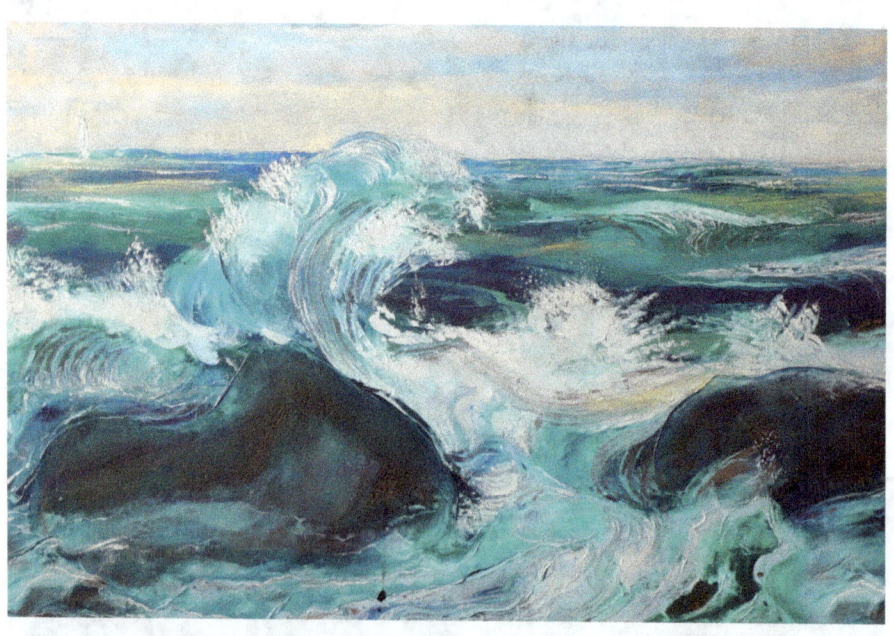

# Like a sand castle

*All made of sand*
*by the seashore,*
*I built it*
*as if with a brush,*
*a beautiful big castle.*

*With more fine sand,*
*I decorated it,*
*with many small stones,*
*I curbed it...*
*And there it was, out of nothing.*

*But it lived briefly,*
*like the day,*
*or the sea wave*
*that comes and goes,*
*slowly on the beach.*

*The evening falls,*
*and on the shore remains*
*a circle of gravel:*
*my essence lived the time*
*of a sand castle.*

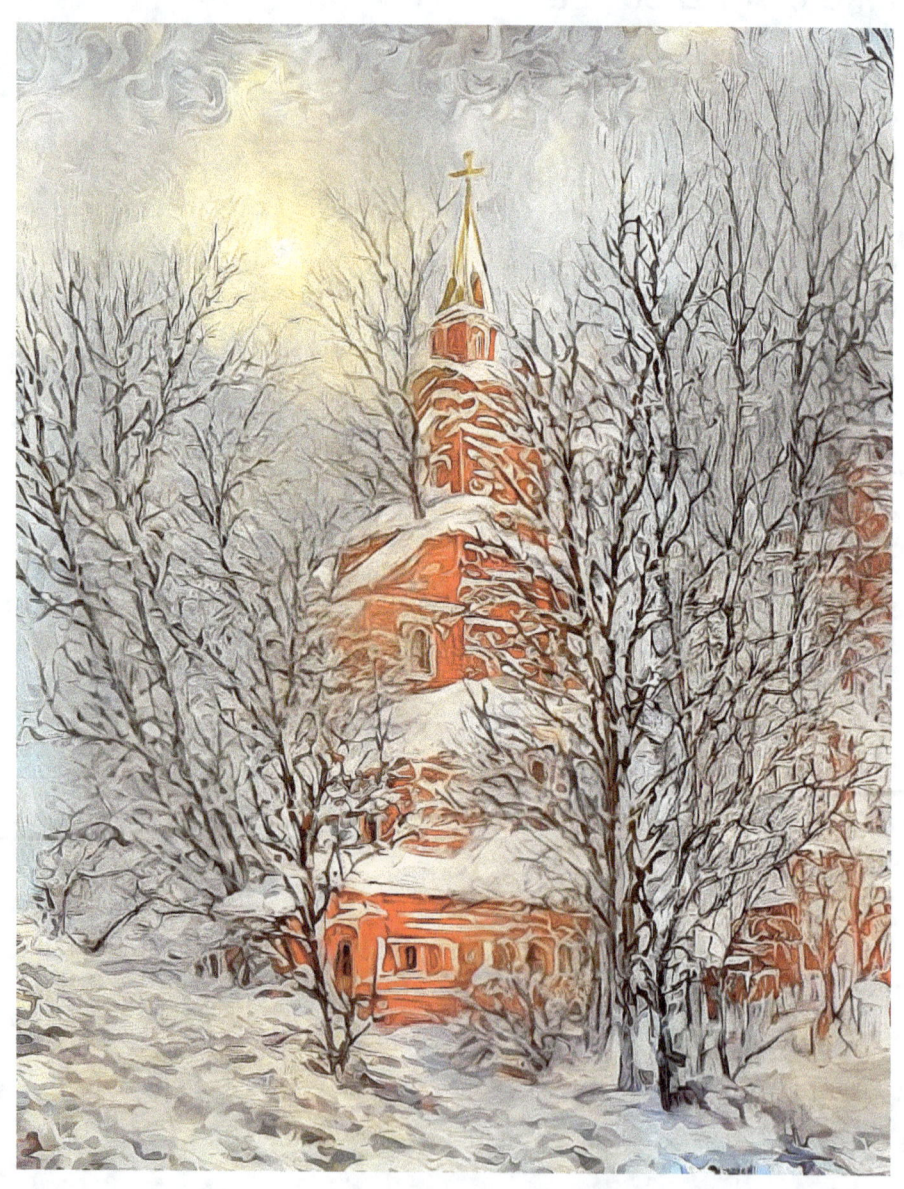

## Renewing

*Like the religious one*
*in her creed,*
*it's the highest expression*
*of a power beyond humans*
*that rules her universe.*

*It must be cosmic,*
*it must be an ecstasy of faith.*
*Christ revealed it*
*the accessible, the available,*
*to everybody charitable.*

*Transform oneself, renew oneself,*
*accept, understand the will.*
*The intuited forces,*
*the images of the event,*
*the archaic historicity of existence*
*behind the apparent now.*

## White

*There, where no longer is a trace,*
*static time is silent.*
*The image appears,*
*white by reflections*
*of silent words.*

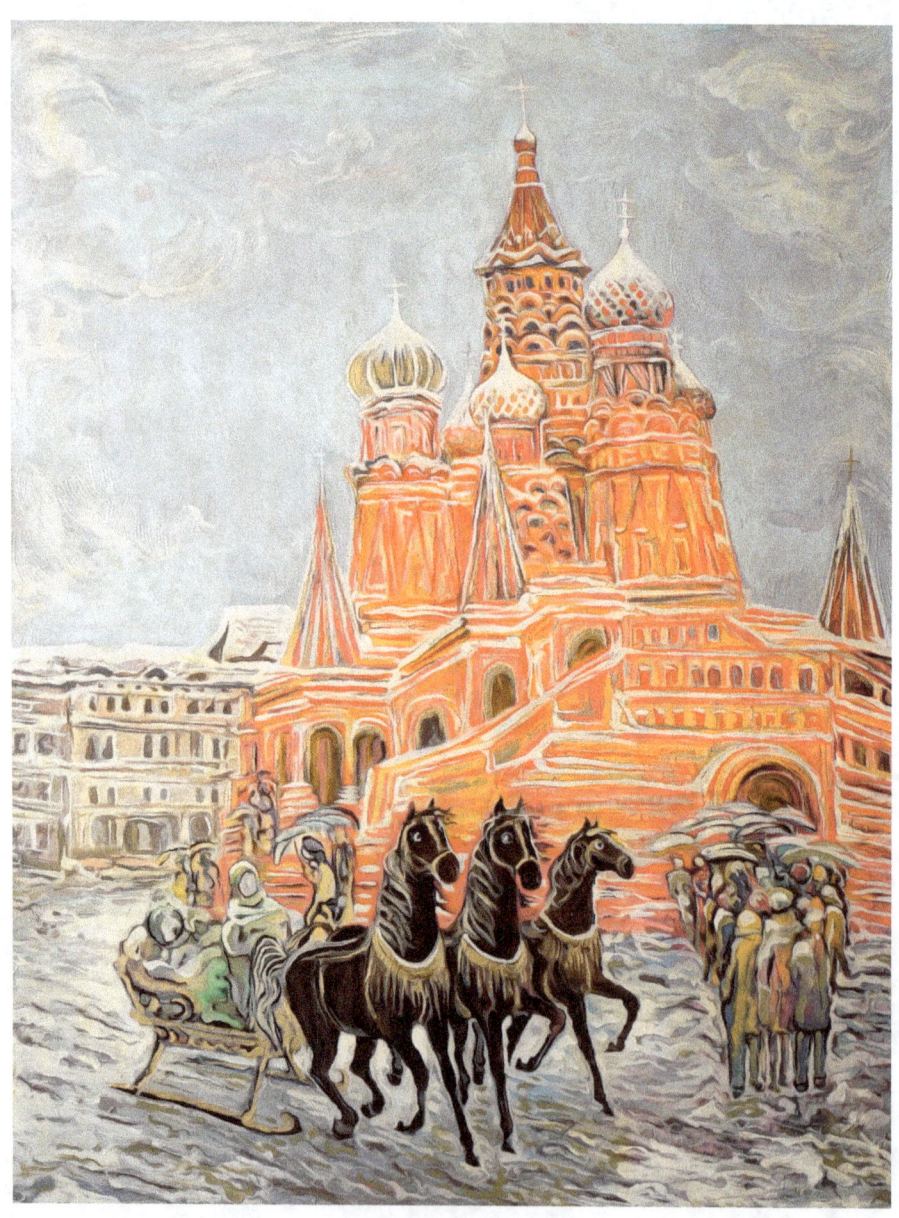

# Song

*My prayer*
*in the dark night,*
*when I see the hidden silence*
*spreading like an oil stain*
*on the waters,*
*parasite damage.*

*You live happily,*
*carefree, unconcerned,*
*unseeing*
*and unhearing*
*the great noise*
*made by the usurper.*

*God is with us*
*in every where and every when...*
*So my song*
*knows and sees that nothing can*
*more than what's done,*
*erase from the true song.*

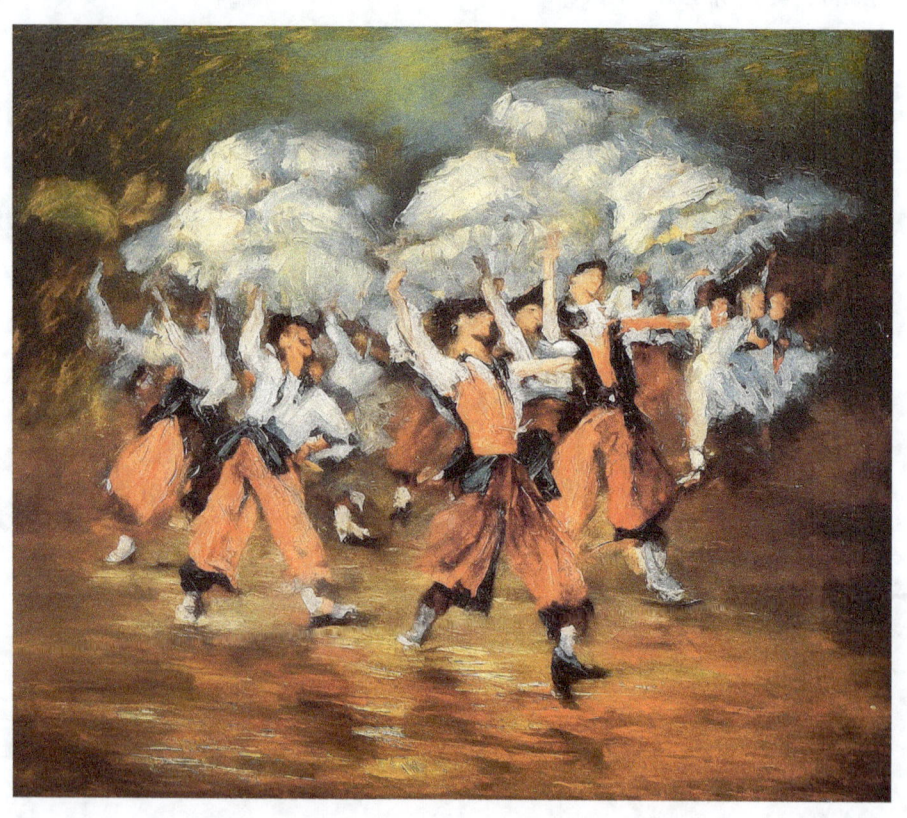

# Transfer

Here's a new blackout of my memory,
you are the mother of all troubles
and of true death.
Oh memory!...

Tones of captured energy
merged with hypnotic apathy,
you transfer her into me,
onto reasons and precise tracks of emotions.

No active, vibrant celebrations,
no joys, no fortunes:
seeds of pain, suffering.
I am late in remembering...
and here comes unconsciousness.

Intermittent memory
of cellular knowledge,
a livid disease in you,
lying passive: go away,
you that hide the true data.

Activate... Encourage and search,
strip them bear and educate the optimus of enthusiasm,
the breath, the peace.

Among goods, love is the greatest.
Be one of those who love the most
and enjoy life.

# Purification

*Flow, cold wellspring,*
*overturning my soul,*
*wash it from its horrors.*
*Valley of great sorrow.*

*Flow quickly, wellspring,*
*move the stone and take me away,*
*rivers flow underneath*
*of voiceless tears.*

*I beg you, wellspring,*
*quench this burning thirst*
*of hatred and revenge, blind*
*from regret, I beg you.*

*In the bed of the night,*
*returned by sweat*
*to the atrocious thought. The hours...*
*it brushes and touches the forehead,*
*the icy breath of death.*

*From sorrow, I sink*
*into your water,*
*and with hands*
*that sweat cold,*
*I count and recount the years.*

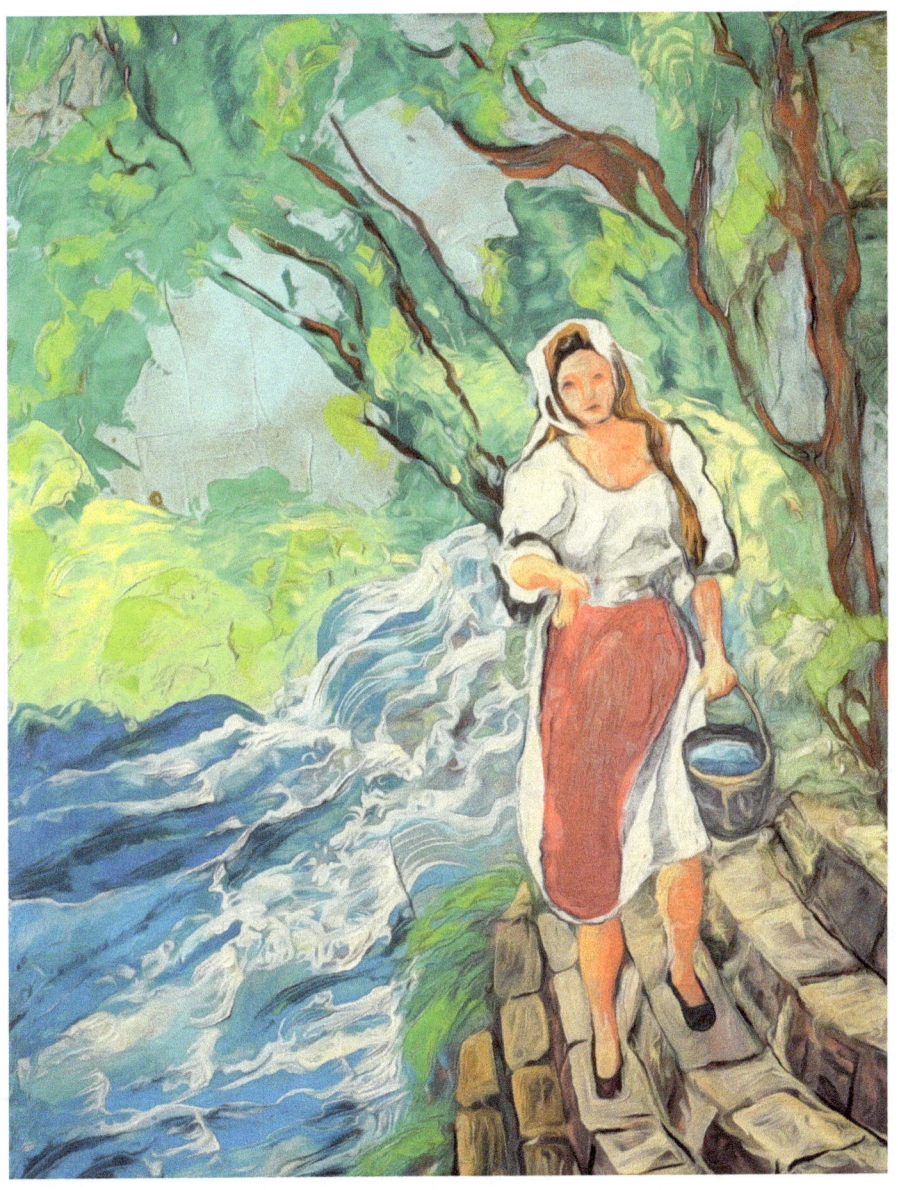

## Reflections

*The glassy gaze*
*mirrors in the water.*
*Petrified is*
*joy by pain.*
*Crystalline is the thought*
*of the old memory*
*returned to me.*

## Dream

*One day in May,*
*my life appeared to me,*
*young and beautiful,*
*in a white dress.*
*What a beautiful dream I dreamt,*
*and as I left you, it left me.*

*She, the young*
*faithful companion, with me*
*walked the road, taking me,*
*the sacred rose of the useless dream.*
*In youth, betrayed I was,*
*and was life that betrayed me.*

*It's strange, I dreamt*
*and dreamt again, and today I can*
*make a dream come true, modify*
*a fact narrated to me.*

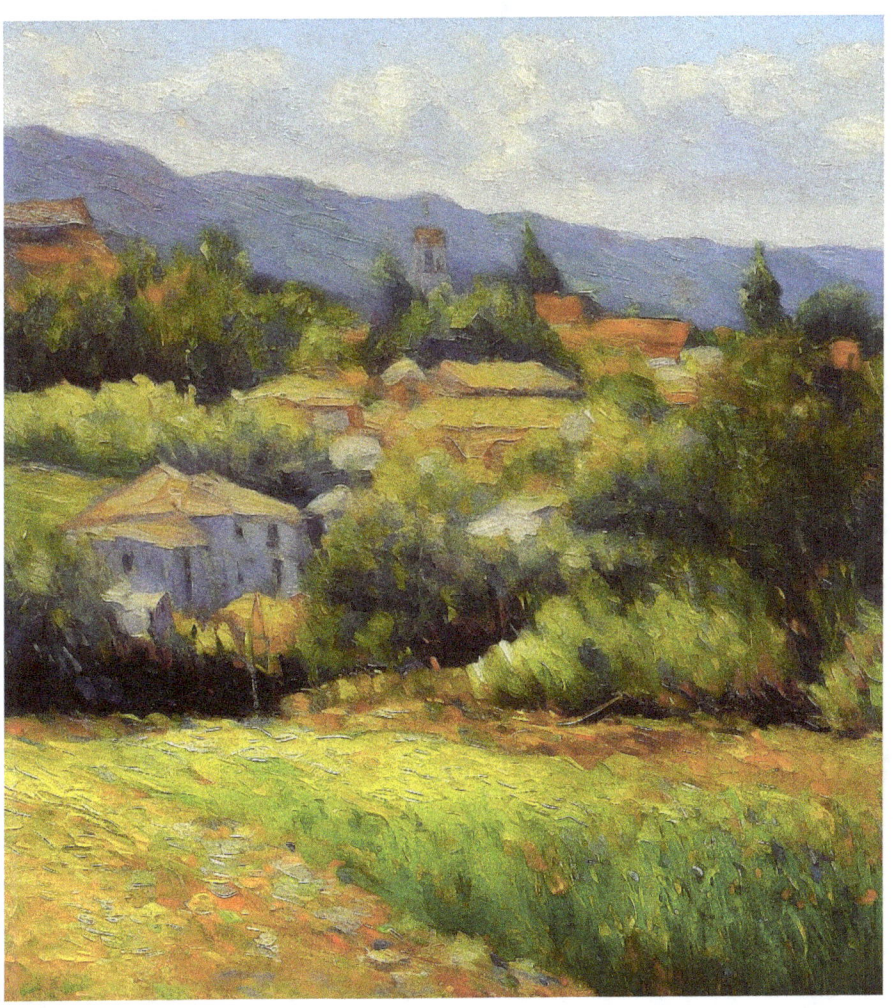

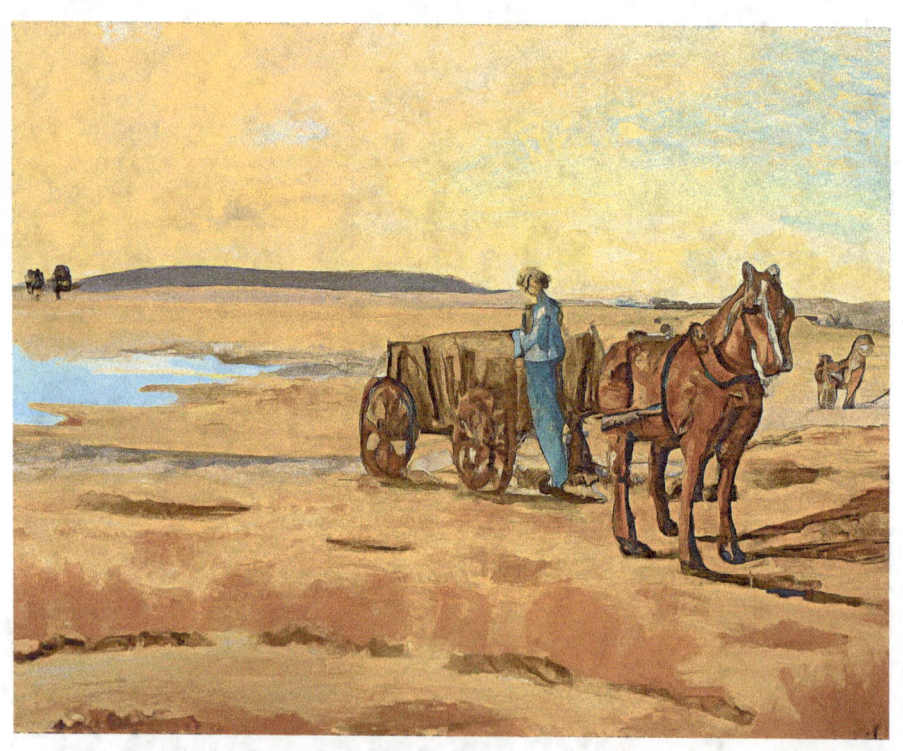

# On the bank of the Prut

Men are threshing,
the wheat in my country,
from fine straws.
Around the posts, in a circle,
they make the horses go around.
Oh! summer that dwells in my country...

On the axle that the tired horses
were dragging,
I mounted next to the man,
very amused
on the shining straw
under the scorching sun.

I went up and down,
as if in a song I glide
marking with my finger women
who separated
the grains in the wind,
from fine straws.

They made their buckets rain,
with hopping grains
on fine sackcloth.
White oxen already plowed
the fields next door,
naked, reaped the wheat
I had first planted for them,
a stork watched me,
in one paw,
from the bank of the Prut.

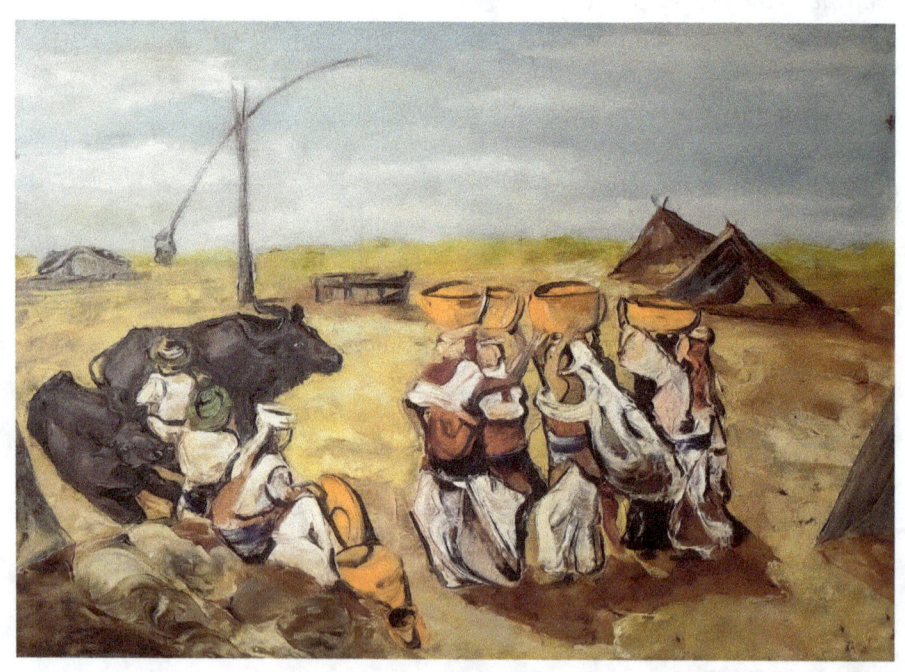

# From under the rocks

Gradually, in the soul,
grew knowledge,
antidote and poison.
From Egyptian expertise to antibodies,
the contempt of will,
cracks, defects,
uncultivated seeds of weeds.

Today, cautious languages,
capable wisdom,
to decongest
exasperating lives,
but we don't start, we stand still.
Universe and human cosmos
emerge like dreams
from beneath the ancient rocks.

The grappling hook,
the pharaoh's eye,
scratches in the past, the gaze,
sick archeology
of genetic plagues.
Leaps into today's time
on the extraordinary steps
of engineering events.

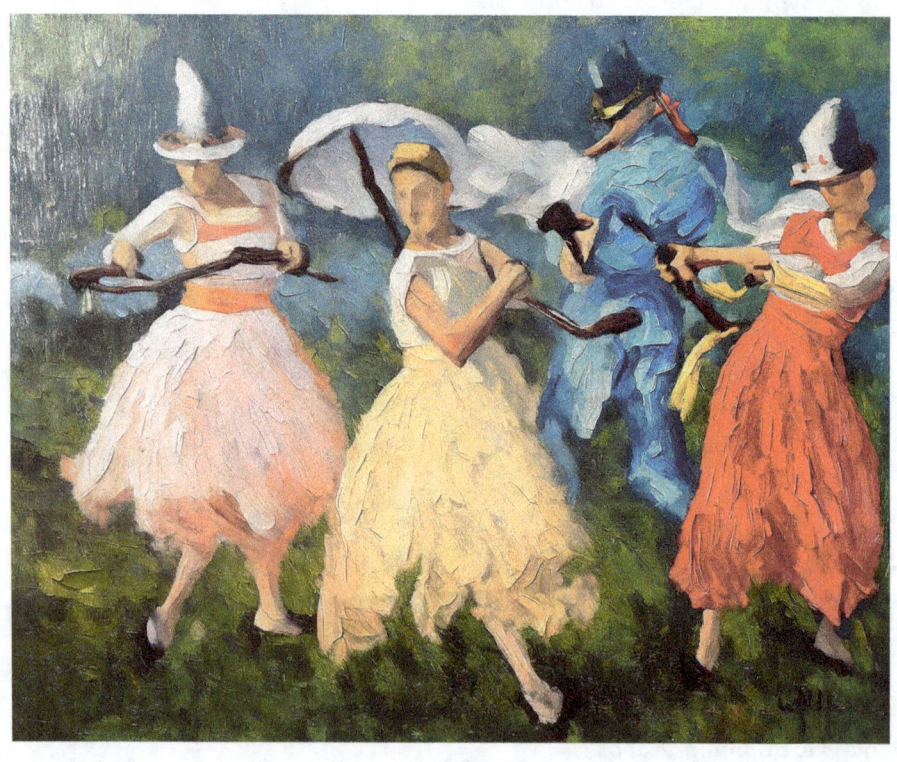

# Friends

*You who know me,*
*you don't know, how much you don't know.*
*Immense is the sky,*
*and immense is the knowledge*
*that never is certainty.*

*Understanding your will*
*might be certainty,*
*but how can you, when,*
*fragile, you bend to time*
*and shake your white hair.*

*Perhaps, yes, there is, it exists,*
*a deep wisdom...*
*Only the heart reads it*
*in each of us,*
*who entrusts it to the mind.*

*It's friendship, it's faith,*
*it's hope in itself,*
*and in everything you do,*
*yes, then you understand me...*
*and you know me, truly.*

# Fear

They felt awe,
it was respect in them.
Only if they touched the robes
they were healed in body
and deep faith arose
on their foreheads.

Suddenly,
immediately,
every source of evil dried up.
Confidences arise,
awes cease,
joys awaken
genes of germination
of deep peace.

# Believe me

Always take courage,
don't be afraid
everything is possible
for those who have faith,
deep faith.

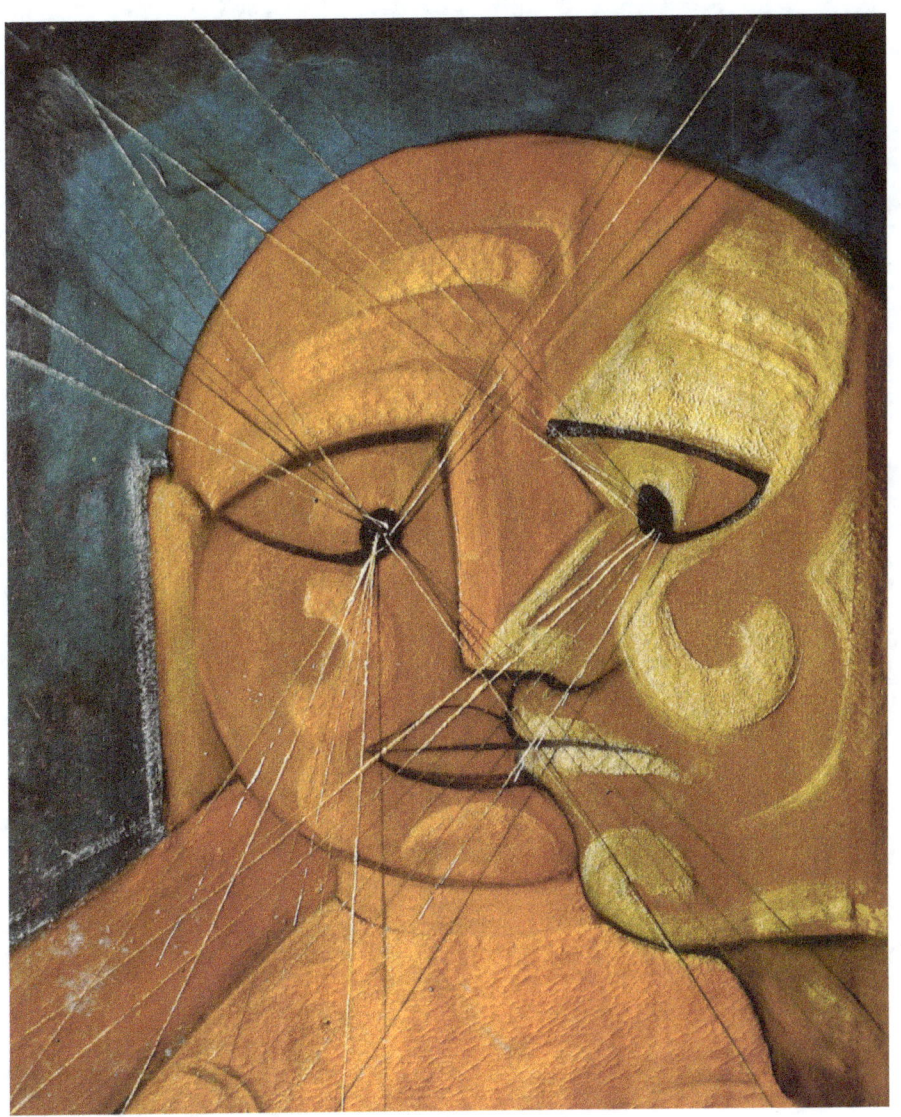

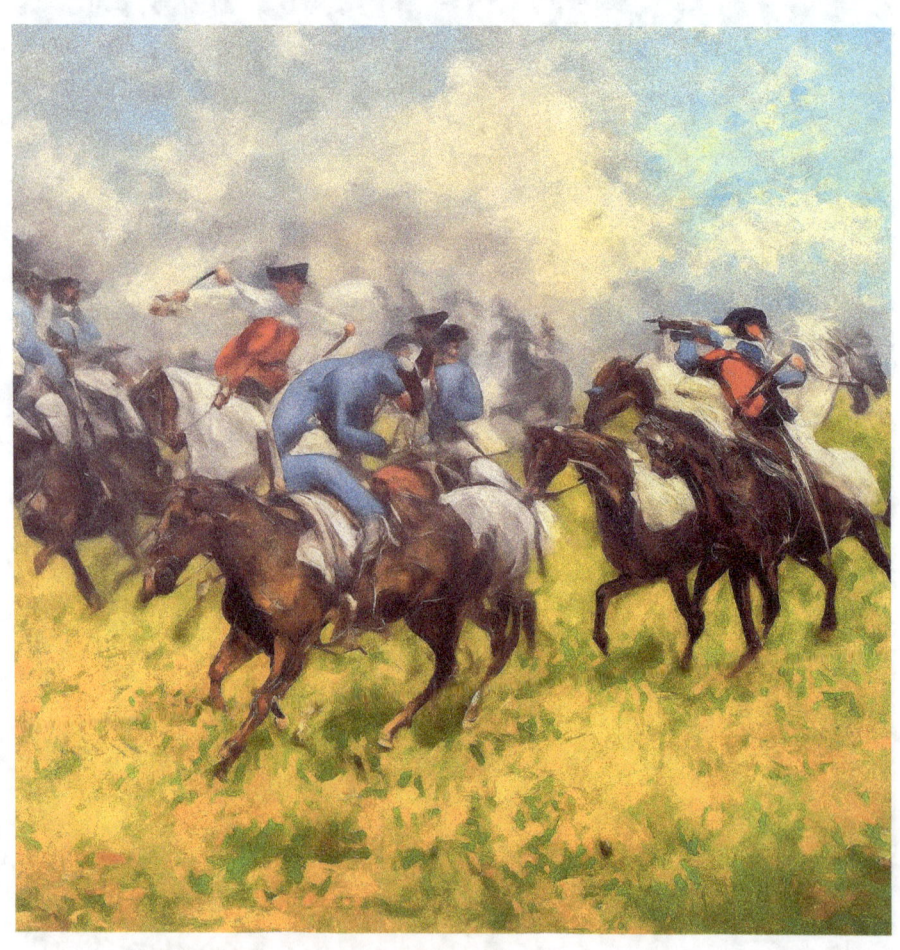

## Gold

*Gold despoilers,*
*gold in which they take delight,*
*considered as silver, nothing,*
*even by young sons.*

*Arid desert regions*
*of the heart,*
*where jackals howl*
*against its dunes.*

*From deferred days,*
*in captivity, gold servants and maids,*
*lie satisfied in sleep.*
*Virtue that fell from the sky,*
*in time you plummeted as gold.*

*Still, you shine like the sun,*
*son of the dawn, sons*
*of hearts that were golden:*
*and one day, the highest throne*
*and not a yoke.*

*The pure hand,*
*outstretched in its action, was creating gold.*
*Fulfilled today, in pride,*
*by the branches that grow*
*in its own false song*
*of despoiling.*

## The first like the last

*The first lights of the day,*
*the last shadows of the night.*
*A sweet sound woke me*
*from a bitter dream I had lived.*

*I look out the window,*
*seeking into the world,*
*what I lost, I think,*
*everything as if doubled,*
*other things paired, and I find it unjust,*
*the dream, that now I have to seek,*
*that I have known,*
*and need you.*

*Why all of this? Perhaps...*
*to have the exact dimension for myself?*
*No... not hypocrisy, presumption,*
*but true and holy truth I demand.*

*White has black, man has woman,*
*opposites in everything,*
*every form of life,*
*a mother, a father,*
*a seed, a fruit.*
*We are far apart in other deceptions,*
*we rotate engaged, or are you dead?*
*You are in the cold earth.*

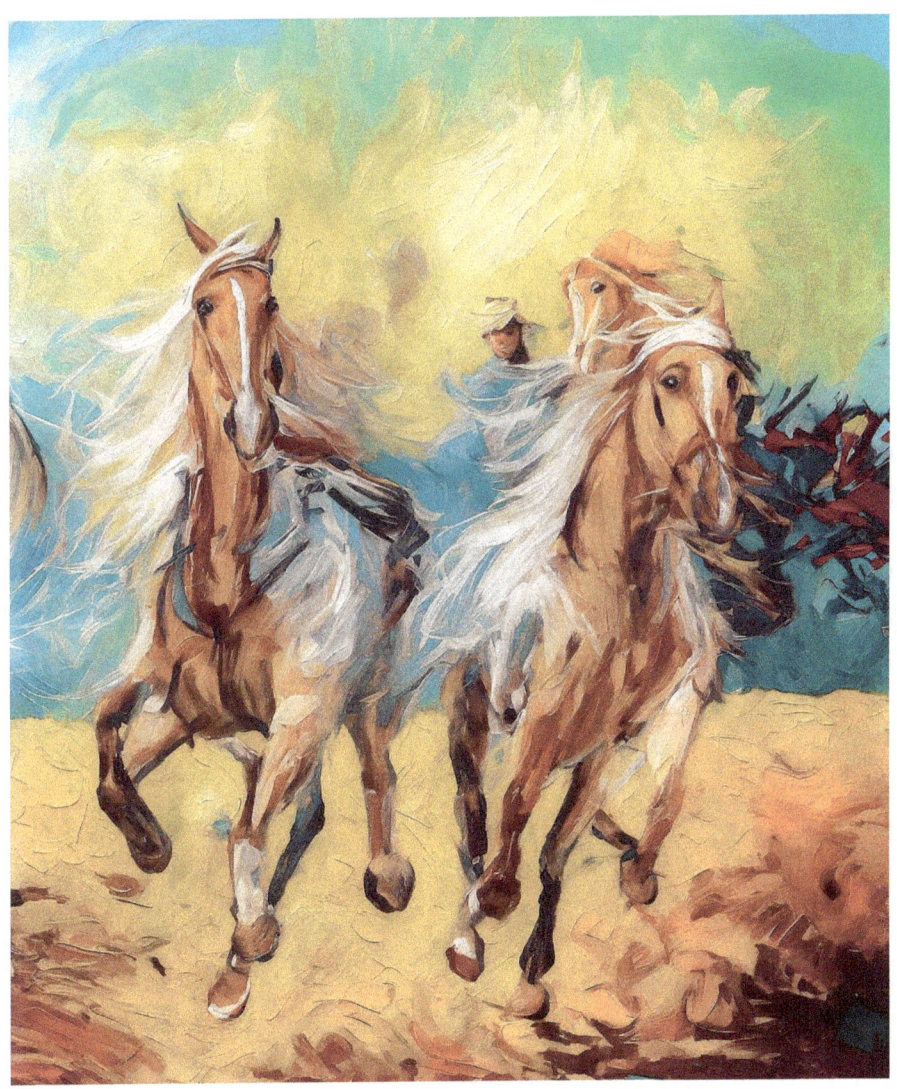

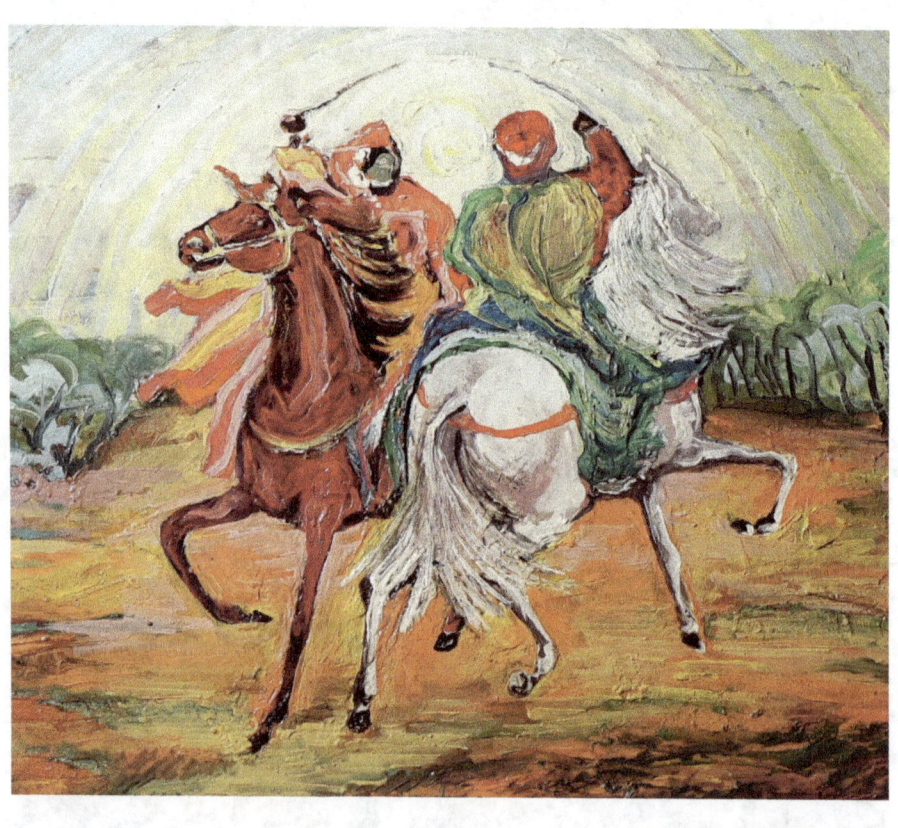

# A tyrant enemy

Still stands it like a condor
on the apex of the last branch.
Does he dominate the landscape
on the leaden background of the sky?

I feel how you would tear apart
this flesh of mine, and personality,
with your fierce rage. Who knows
why you've been persecuting for a lifetime.

I had a green hair,
I stretched my arms to the sky when I was young
to magnify the created
and its immense greatness.
Did you see me, did you lean
on that branch and pecked me, why?

Useless winds, bending to the ground
to shake you off I did,
I broke my branches, all the leaves
fell. Now I envisage
looking for a hiding place for the soul
while you wait to have the carcass.

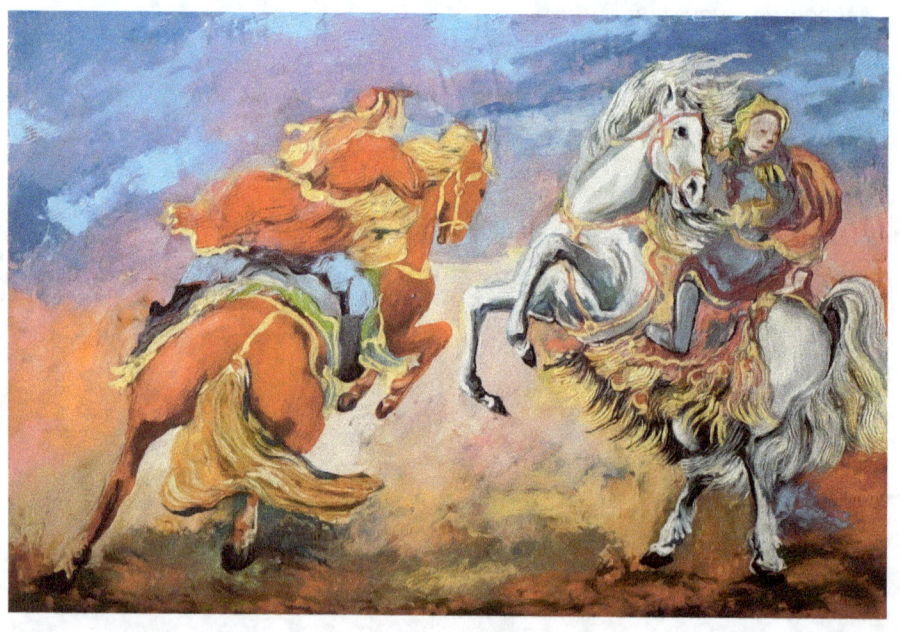

# Help

*Help the wind,*
*saga of youth,*
*burnt breath on the skin.*
*Lost entrusted children,*
*others found and saved.*

*Go help, run.*
*He didn't want to talk,*
*took his breath away,*
*that harsh, merciless world.*

*Wild slaughter.*
*Depressions and highs,*
*swings of life tones*
*of faded moods.*

*Torment and mixture*
*that explodes the hours*
*and moments of life.*
*Pulse, breath, and light,*
*life of the world, help.*

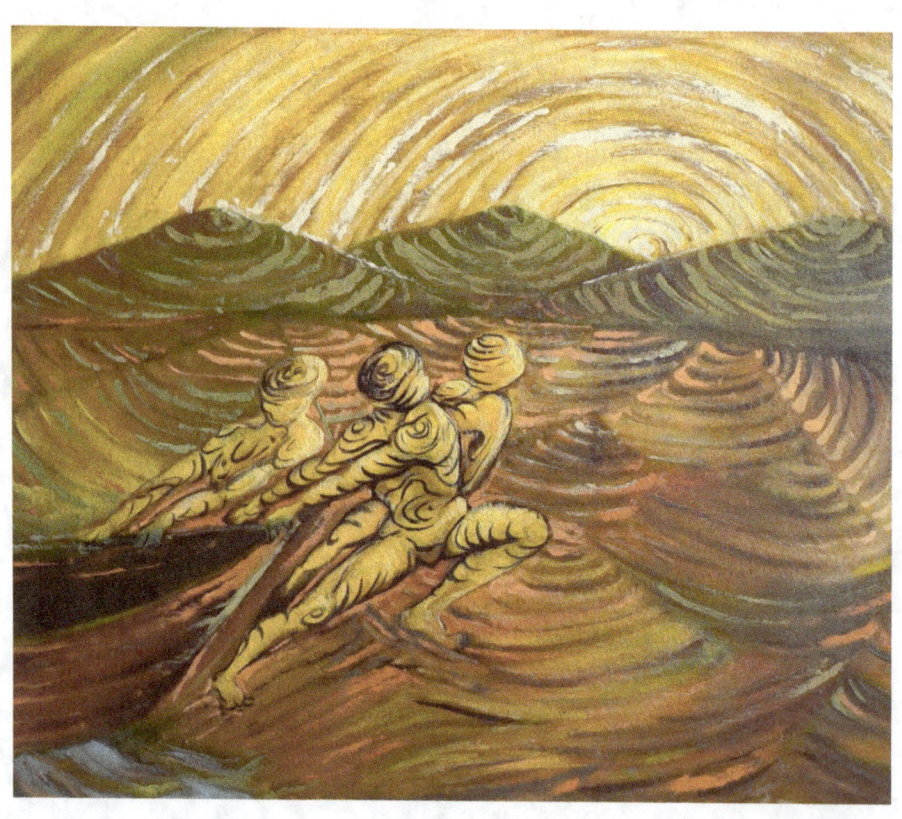

# Whirlwind

*Here comes the hurricane,*
*with a whirlwind of thistles at the center,*
*seeds and things fly,*
*like chaff in powder,*
*the roar of the clouds*
*makes a tumult.*

*The downpour of powerful waters,*
*frosted hail flow.*
*Tumultuous, they chase each other,*
*pushed by the wind the black*
*and white clouds.*

*They thunder, flash,*
*roaring in the distance.*
*Nature is full of energy*
*and terror.*

*Buzzing wings of birds,*
*of joyful bees and insects,*
*return to fly*
*in the cleared sky.*

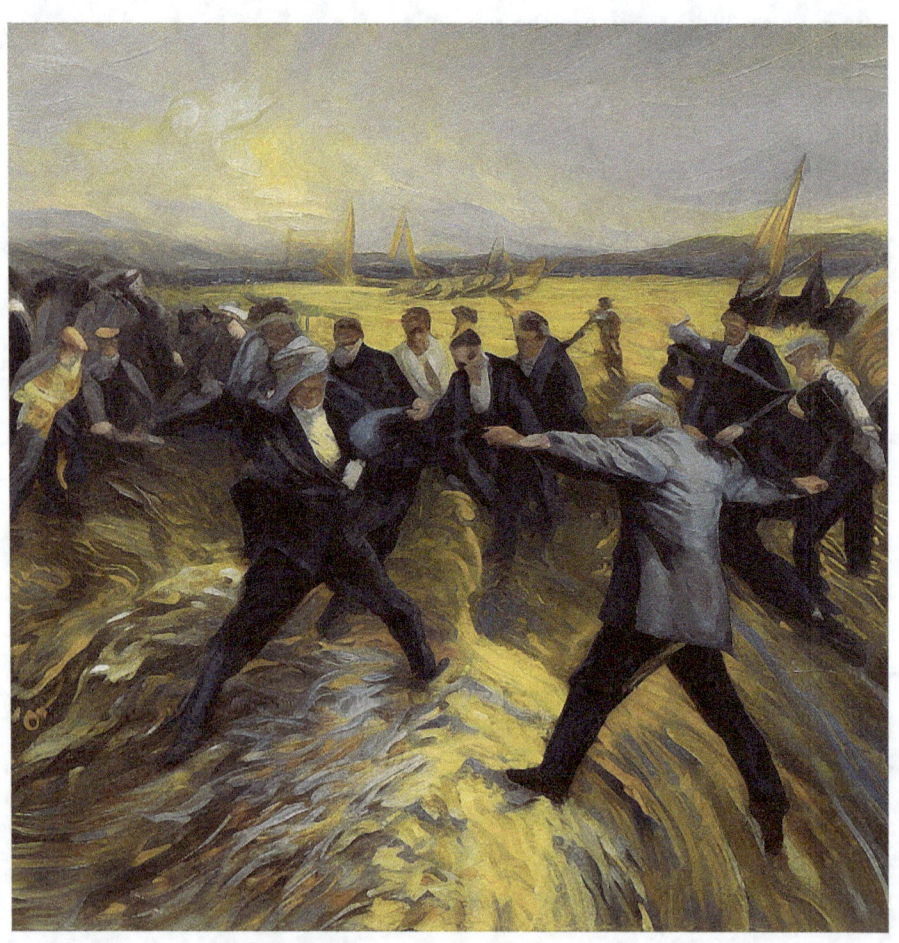

# Funny

You are the funny human being,
who suffers
his post-war century.

A complicated world,
Aberrant its own existence,
bored,
a subdued tone of the plagiarized
with not his own data and facts.

The enslaved mind, made funny
by the elusive inspiration.
Return to mind
where you have a gift
a disenchanted prize.

Generous possessions
talents and impulses
of vast memory seas.

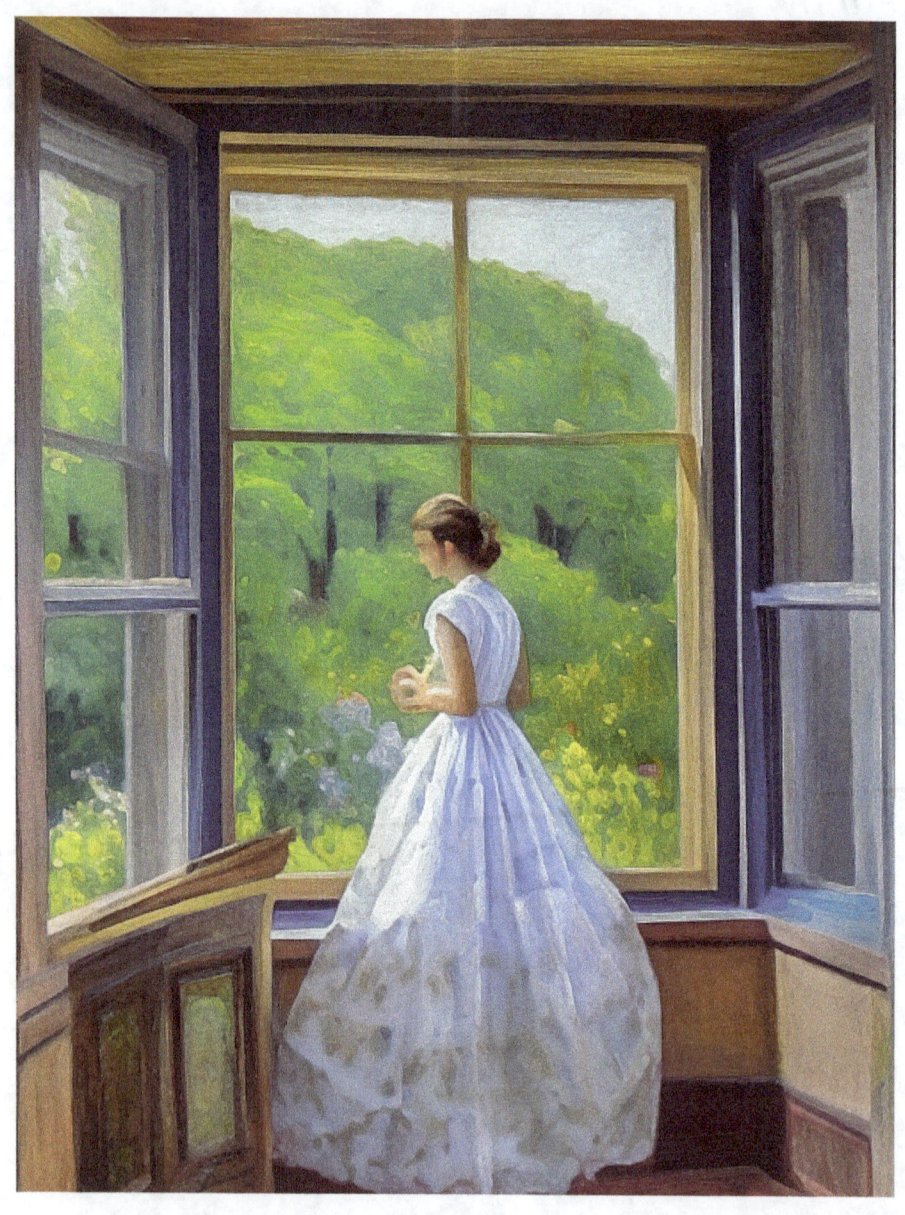

# Waiting

*Oh... faith, where are you, and I can't feel you,*
*stay with me, remain with me,*
*until the warm breath tarnishes the glass.*

*Don't leave me without hope.*
*We will be alone to sum things up*
*at the bottom of the end of days.*

*Waiting has a limit,*
*or it's suffering.*
*It begins with the sunrise*
*and fade with the evening.*

*Free your free will and determination*
*from the lead of waiting,*
*which spies on you punctually through the windows,*
*without knocking on the door.*

*Waiting is your friend,*
*but it's your enemy.*
*When hope leaves you*
*for what you crave with faith,*
*weigh and discern the futility.*

## Rhythms

*Even nowadays*
*great happenings take place.*
*Unthought forces, effects,*
*causes and behaviors,*
*demonstrate glimpses*
*and rhythms of rhythms,*
*going in crescendo*
*and decrescendo, jumping.*

*There are intuitions,*
*calculations of their cells*
*that God has saved, defended,*
*and purified.*

*Nothing can disturb it anymore,*
*strike that consciousness*
*it rises above*
*the unspeakable sufferings,*
*floats, dominates.*

*On wings of feathers*
*that golden thread flies,*
*it flies over the death wounded*
*by unconscious injury.*

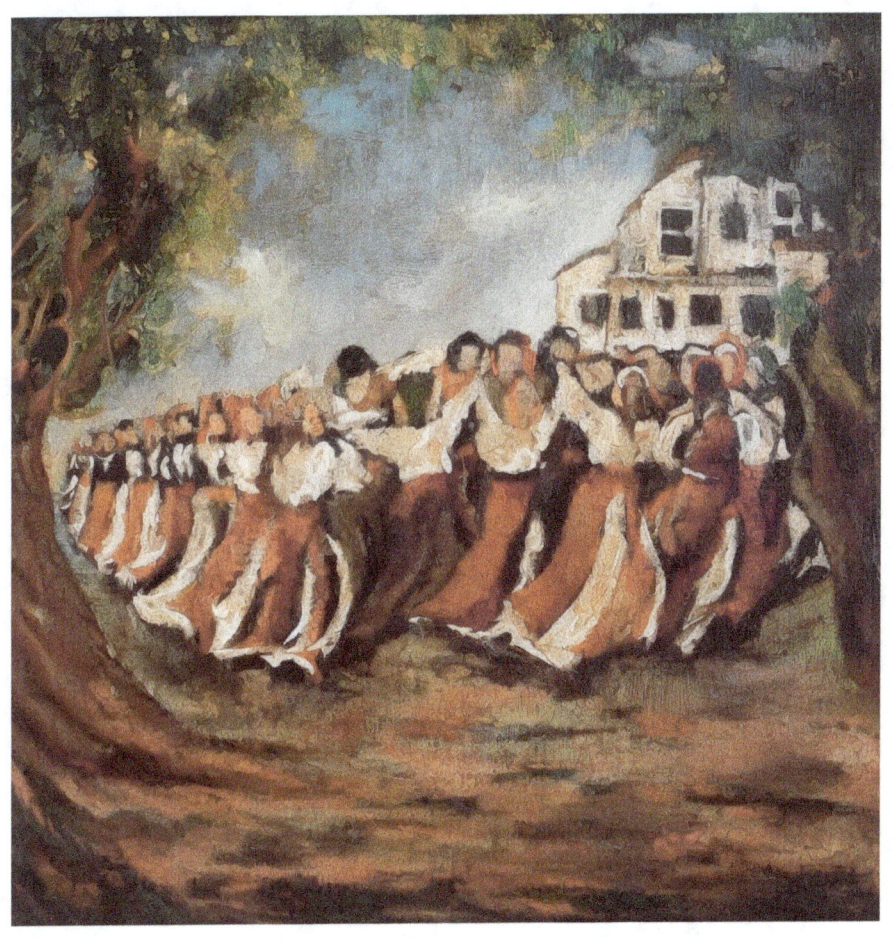

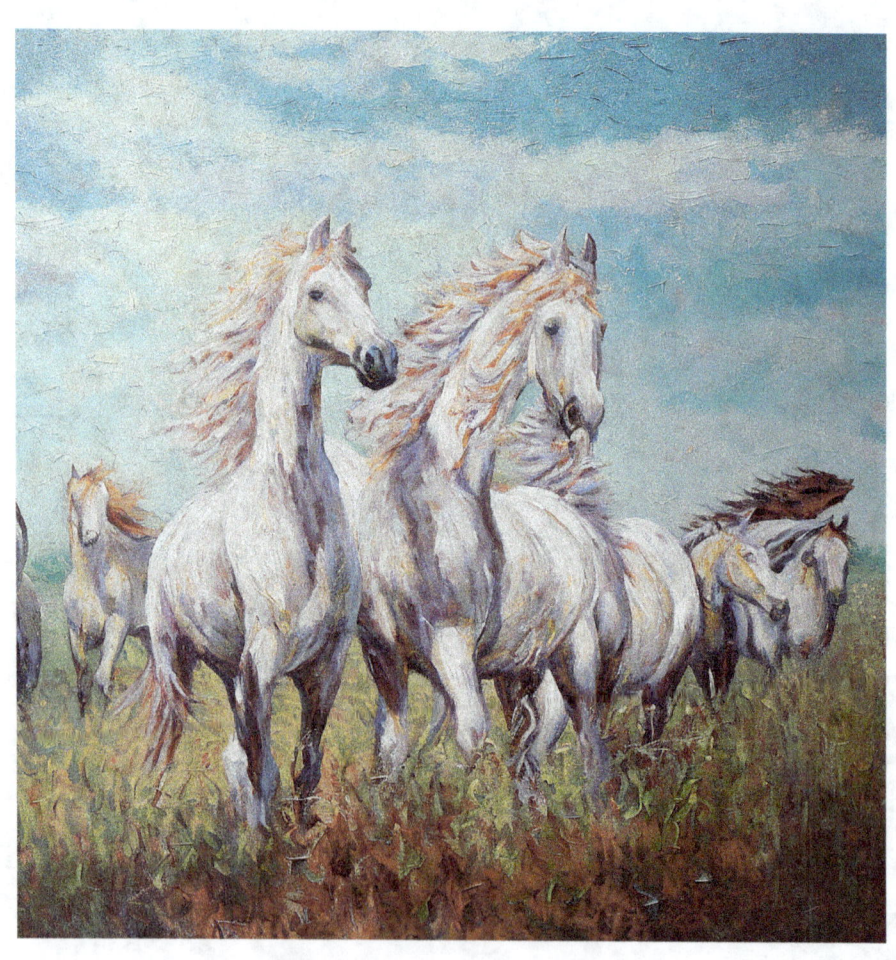

# Hunt

In the woods, the fierce shouts
of the beaters boiled,
I miss that freshness
persecuted by the noise.

The ambush, my friends!
It's everywhere you are.
Enemies. They have spread nets...
they run, and I run defenseless.

Bowing your head to the stake for hours,
you will, unwillingly,
with pain and so much horror,
with me, joining them.

The cries in the woods. Oh...!
You take away any pleasure from life
drop by drop, is exhausted
the futile struggle of existence.

Tired resignation.
Today, the white death
will set us free,
it will sign our glassy eyes
for eternity.

## The orbit

*A solar disk.*

*A genius sublimates man.*
*Rich in ideas, I engage,*
*aiming my arrow*
*toward a big-bang.*

*Dance in the sun*
*under the blooming almond trees,*
*watch joyful the orbit*
*of the results of light.*

## Ray

*Kiss me, spring sun,*
*hold me tight, you who warm*
*distant lands; because,*
*I feel the blood in my veins*
*melt into fluid.*

*Stay a moment longer*
*to love me*
*with your rays*
*in this brief sweet*
*spring season.*

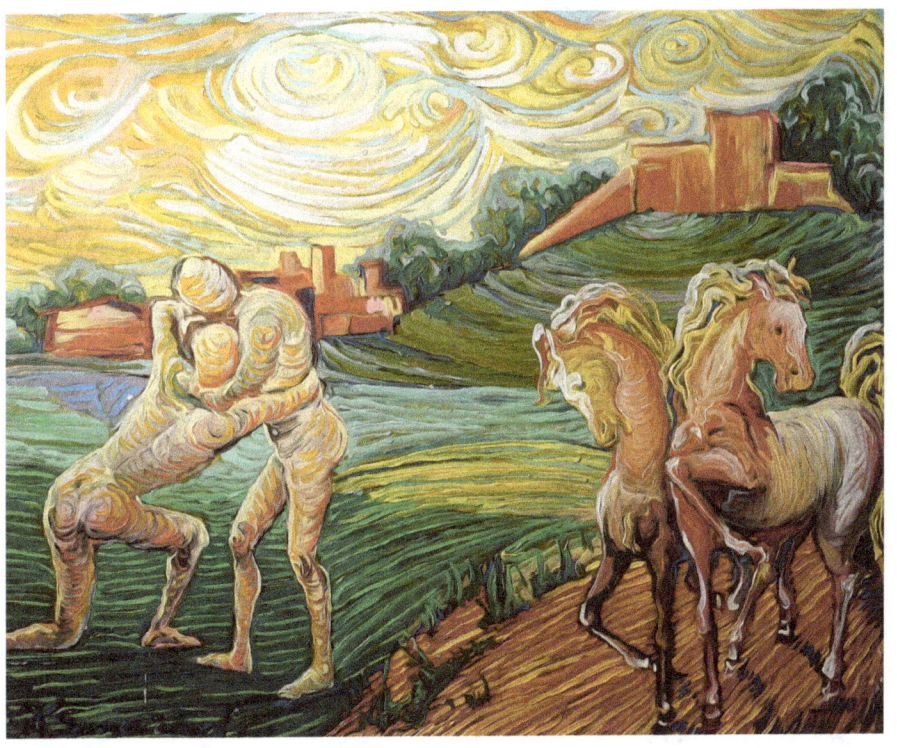

# In front of the fire

Shivers shake me
as I suddenly realize and look:
autumn rages, the wind
sweeps through the countryside. Desert...

Shake the dry leaves
that flutter in the valley
as if dismayed,
settling on the ground.

Here and there, traces of ash,
black tar from the fireplace,
marked by the oxen's plow,
the wounded and turned earth.

It awaits peace, weary,
the peace of white snow,
frost and mist
in sight, haze.

No more drops of dew,
from the brook, warm air vapors.

Long nights without stars,
the wind whistles, lashes the flames.

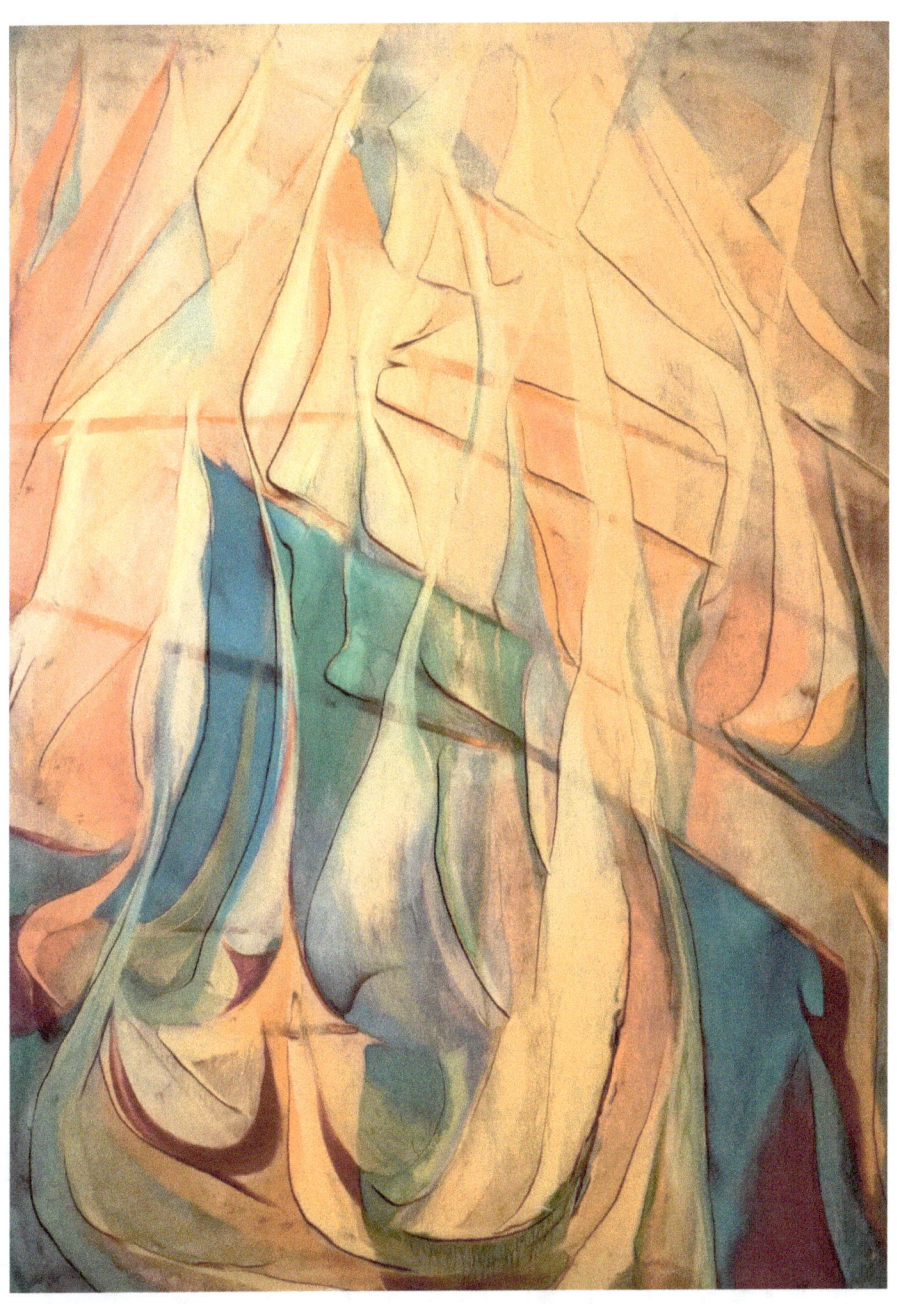

# Distraction

*There was in a meadow,*
*a red rose bud,*
*and a pink daisy*
*asked it to marry.*

*Not out of pride,*
*but out of distraction*
*the rose bud didn't answer,*
*but took some time to think.*

*The sorrowful daisy, then,*
*with another white one got married.*

*Now that the rose lies withered,*
*grieving, she impatiently looks,*
*at the white blanket of the daisy rose*
*that extended around her,*
*remarried her children.*

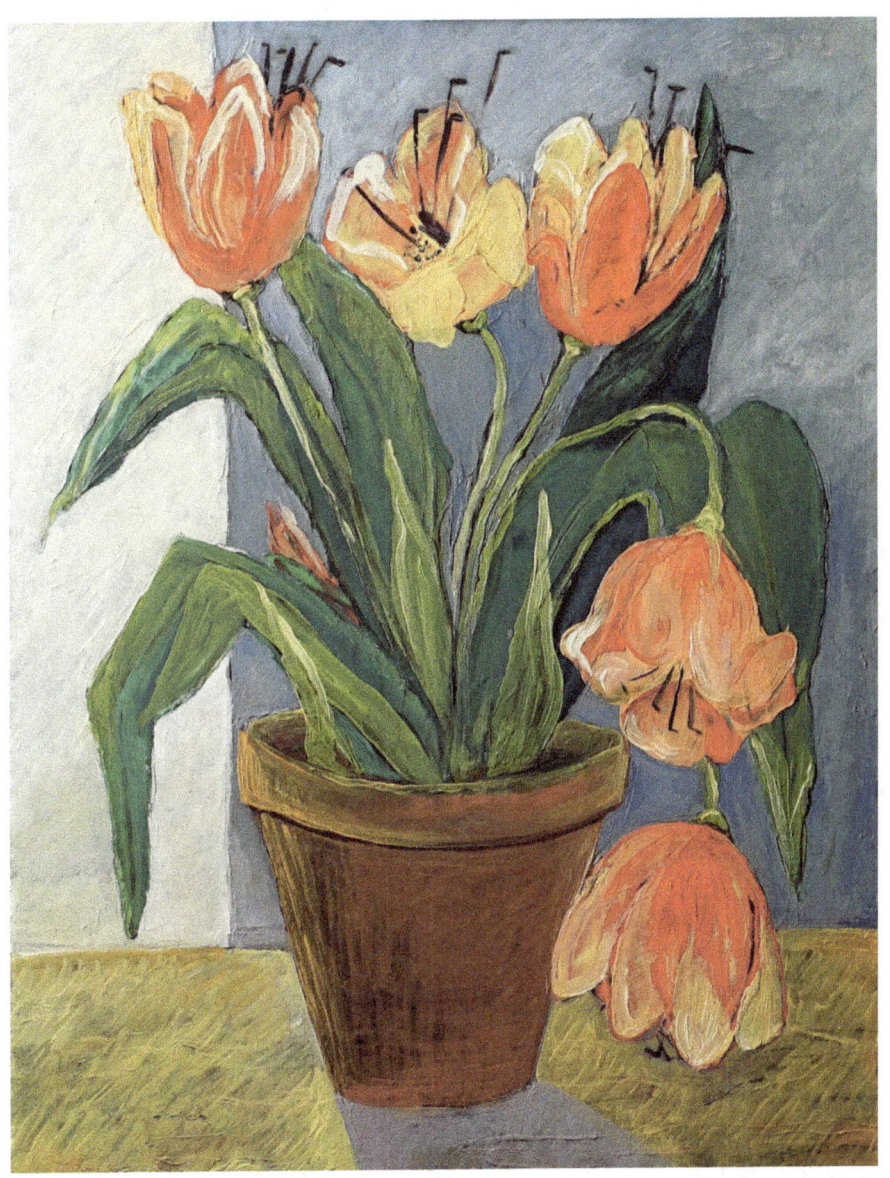

## Live today

Just by thinking
the soul trembles,
the heart beats strongly,
and the joy hurts
for fear of what comes next.
A new spring,
love always sighs.

These lonely nights
never end, lulled
like when you, father,
took care of us. Today,
kneeling,
dragging the step
one after the other.

Sleep in one breath and,
get up directly on your feet
even before opening your eyes.
With weariness, share
life together with everyone, equal.

From problems aged
by uncomfortable things, various,
enclosed in jewel cases
by sealed mouths.
Complained...

Around me last only
investigative looks,
of the unknown navigating.

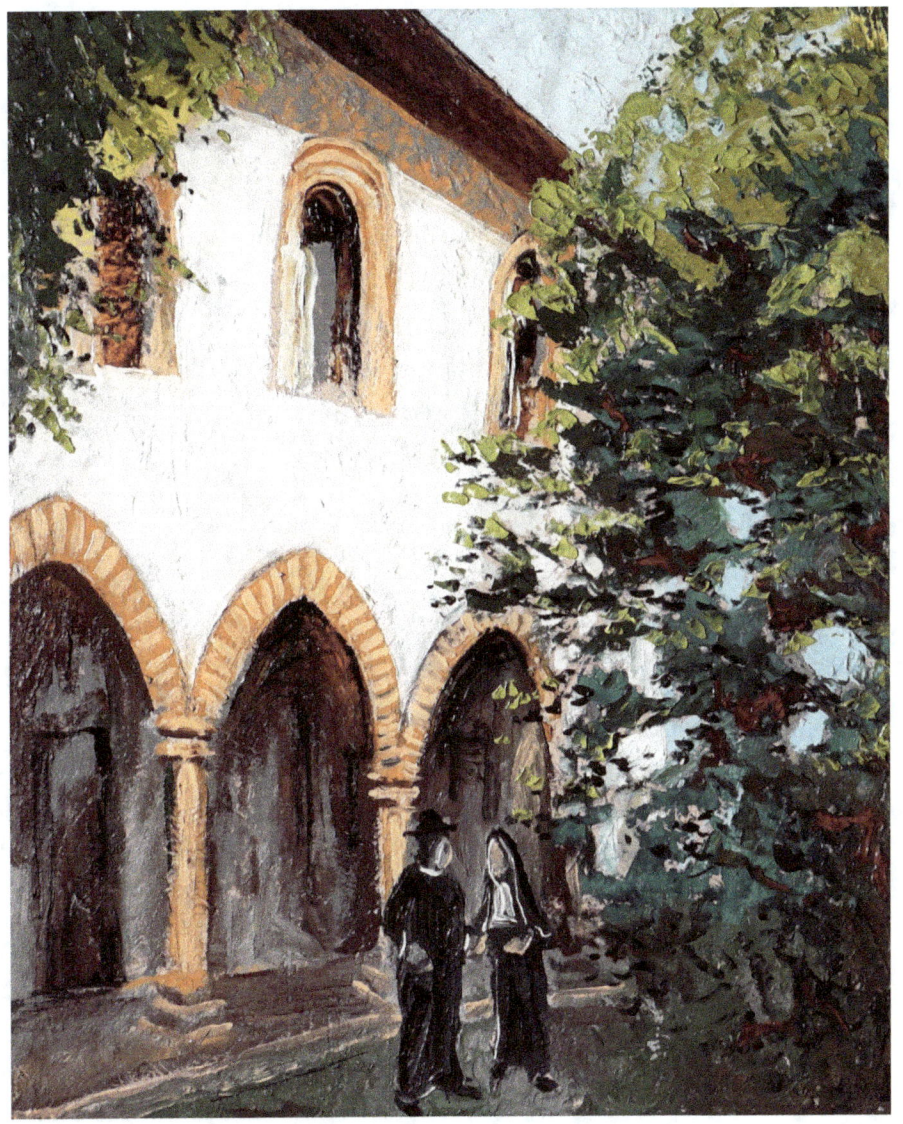

## The light of vespers

*Silent loneliness*
*crosses my path,*
*thinking is nothing,*
*but finding you and seeing you...*
*breaks the heart.*

*How many images crowd*
*the dome of this starry sky,*
*without the moon,*
*without planning tomorrow.*

*I feel warm blood*
*flowing in the veins...*
*and it's warmer than ever.*

## They said

*Everything to everyone they said,*
*she's dear, she's beautiful, very beautiful.*
*They spied on me, they watched me,*
*they flattered me.*

*I said, "I am poor."*
*Destiny disappeared with them*
*who kissed my hand,*
*and turned the corner.*

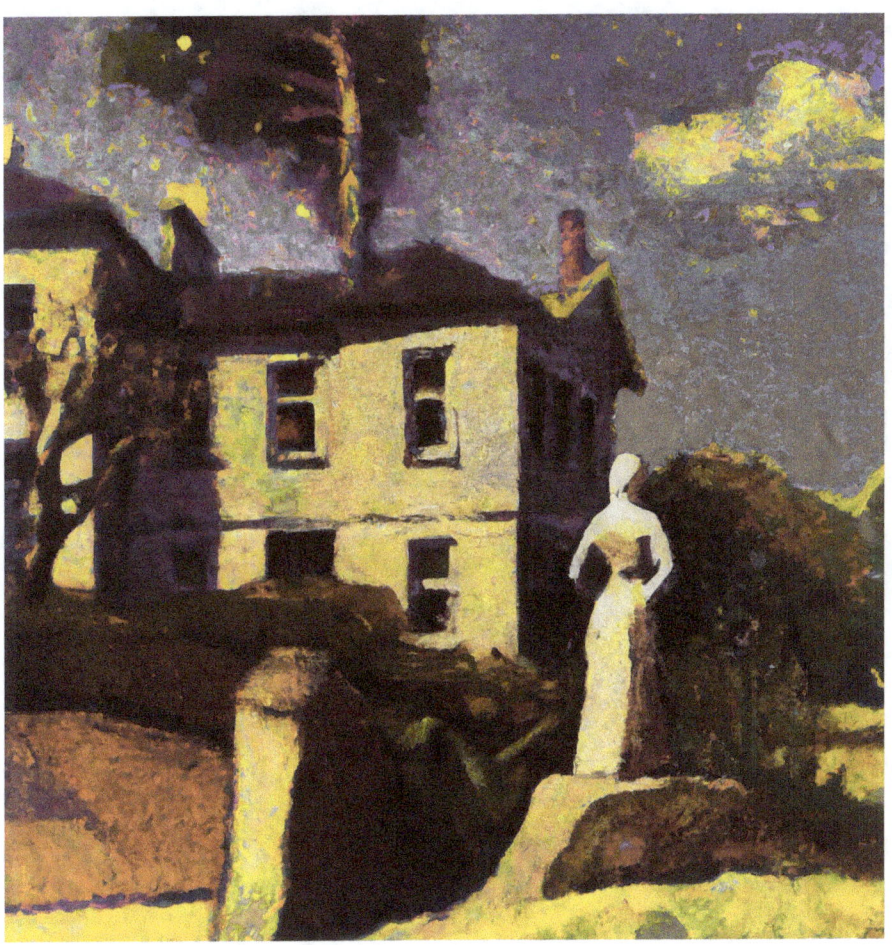

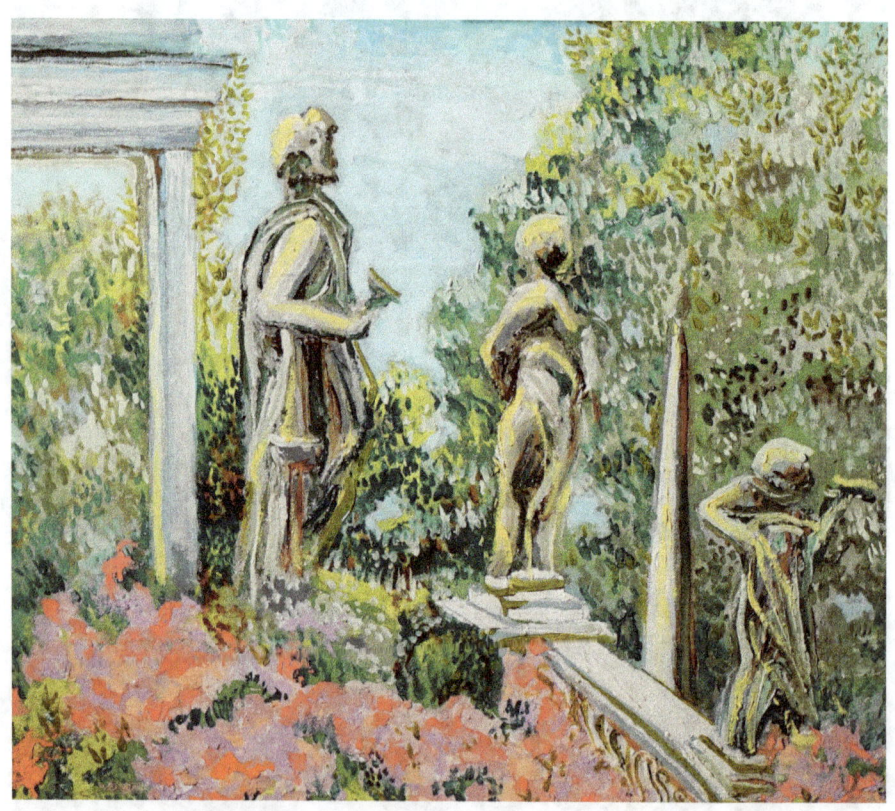

# *Art image*

*The wind whispers*
*among the poplars.*
*Art, I love you.*

*A breath of air*
*vibrates gently,*
*fragrant and warm.*

*On this hill, I wait it*
*in the shade*
*of the olive tree I paint.*

*Among the silver,*
*sibylline leaves,*
*brushstrokes of shining oil*
*escape.*

*The air trembles, silence.*
*The harmony of the spirit*
*glides to reach*
*Into your harbor.*

# *Earth*

*Oh mother earth,*
*oh brother sky,*
*that embrace*
*the laying things,*
*under your dark night wings.*

*In this accomplice hour,*
*naked flesh rises.*
*Loving arms,*
*like blooming stems,*
*toward a gloomy sky.*

*The silence of dawn*
*once again descends*
*with static light,*
*over the violet wake.*

*It softens, and I stretch*
*my sore body.*
*The mind*
*is blurred by sleep.*

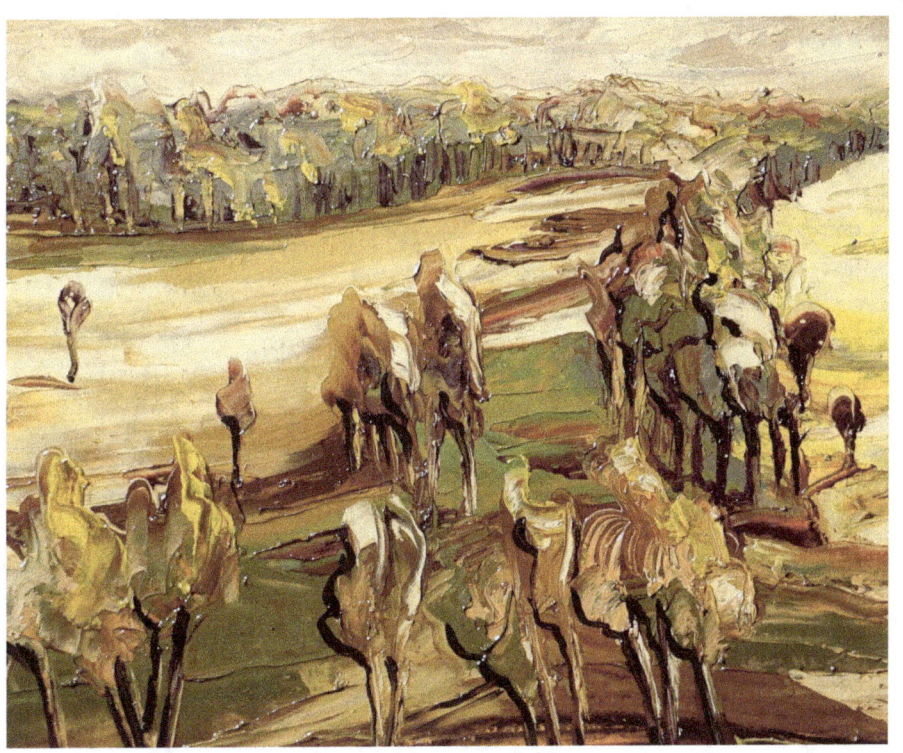

## Sunset

I wish to be young
to make you live,
relive the infinite.

See that one does not stand
still on thoughts.
I want to distract you a bit,
a little, I think.

You must,
you seem dimmed.
Oh... who dims you a little
little by little...

Still, always here in front,
it hurts me to see you, I observe
your years, counting
them: together they are so much,
in the sunset hour.

## Moan

You moan in words,
you cry of poetry,
born between these blank sheets.

You are a dictated text
made by destiny that rages
if you don't become aware.

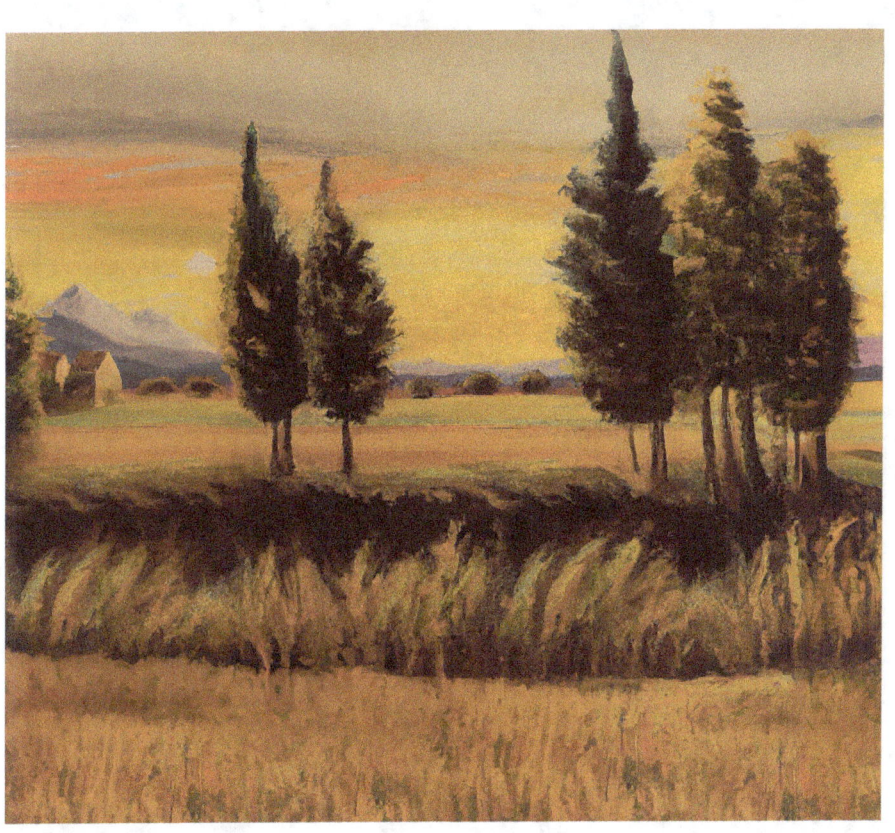

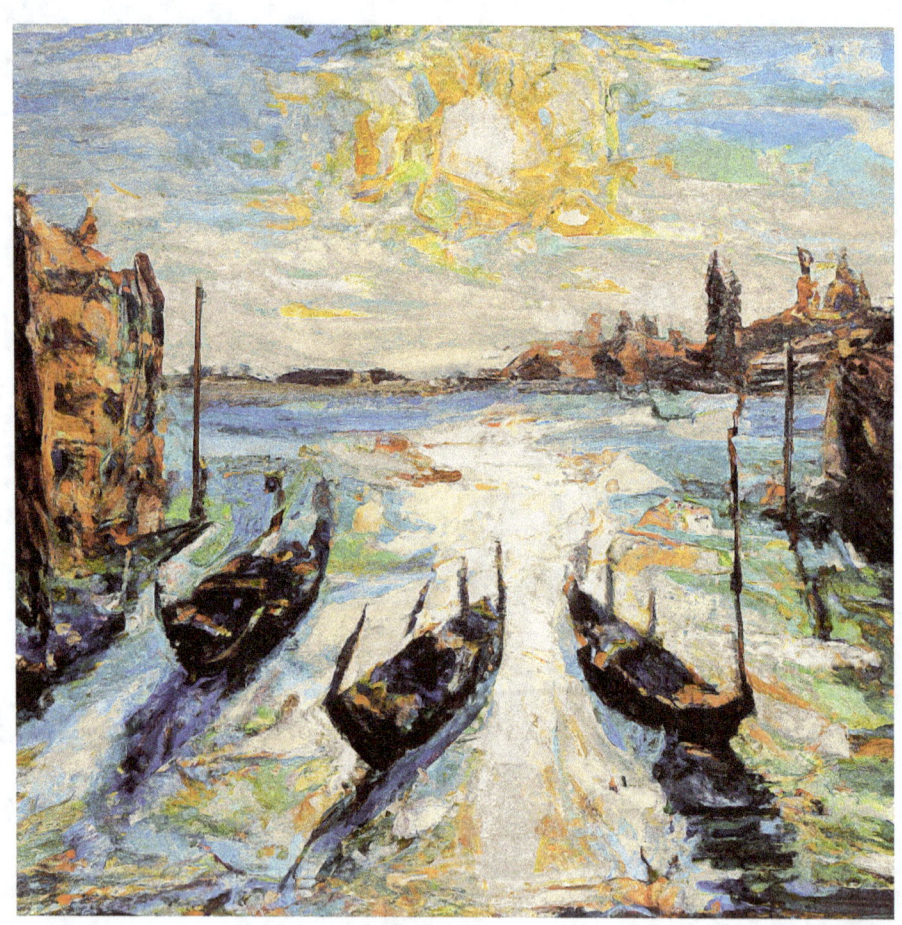

# Time blends

*It varies from hour to hour,*
*from day to day,*
*but I am happy.*

*Time bends*
*on my back,*
*but my stairs ascend*
*step by step,*
*slowly towards serenity.*

*The future goes up*
*always more open,*
*where the wind's flow*
*wanders for me.*

*They float around, I know,*
*dark-shadows causes...*
*I understand, they have always been there,*
*they warn me:*
*caution.*

*Jump the ditch*
*at the right time,*
*in the curve of time*
*that bends and explains the facts.*

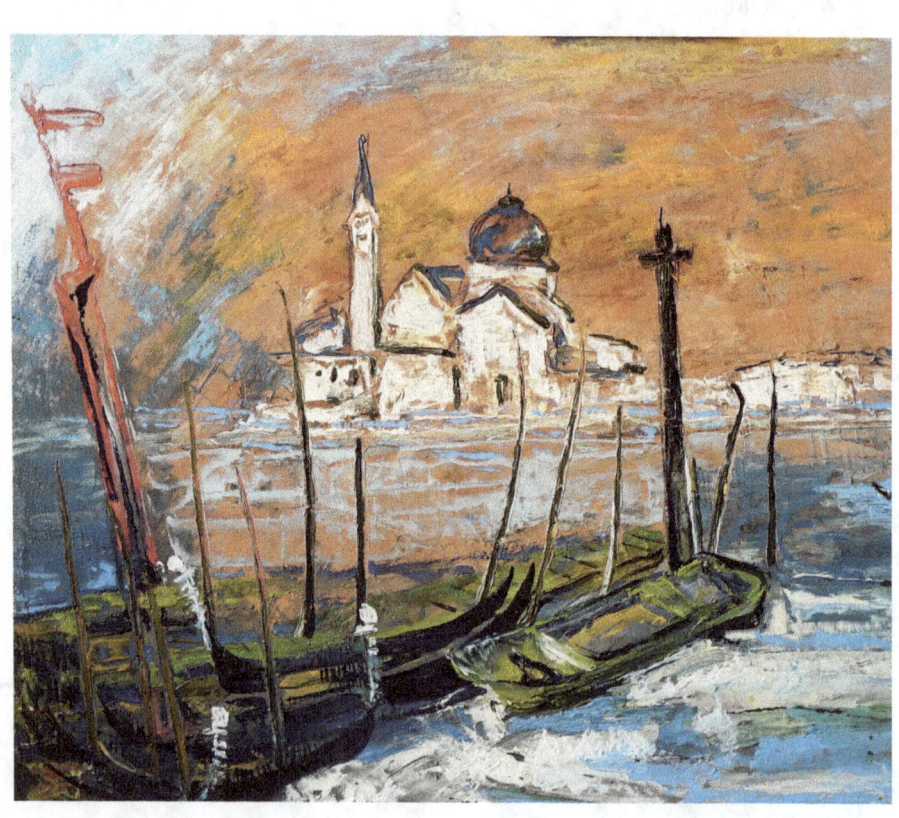

# To never see you again

*I would like to recover*
*from confiding in you.*
*Everything I know,*
*everything you know,*
*has been useless.*

*I don't regret what lived,*
*what little you liked to give me,*
*and losing those joys*
*that you called peaceful*
*with common words.*

*I'm sorry only to meet you,*
*to give me the opportunity to remember*
*my failure*
*when I confided in you*
*and made you pleased.*

## Ciociaro tree blooms

*Like the tree of life,*
*there, where May does not delay,*
*facing the scorching*
*of the already advanced summer,*
*where the trees are rich*
*in shade.*

*Where the obscure privilege*
*of every day,*
*dips its hostile hands*
*into destiny.*

*Only a seed:*
*a whole orchard is not needed*
*to overcrowd misfortune*
*and eat stale leftovers*
*in many hungry and tired.*

*If it is worth it... to reward and*
*immortalize love,*
*transmit respect,*
*embellish the concept,*
*the body, the look.*

*Living freely together,*
*loving without chains imposed*
*by tracks of love and hygiene.*

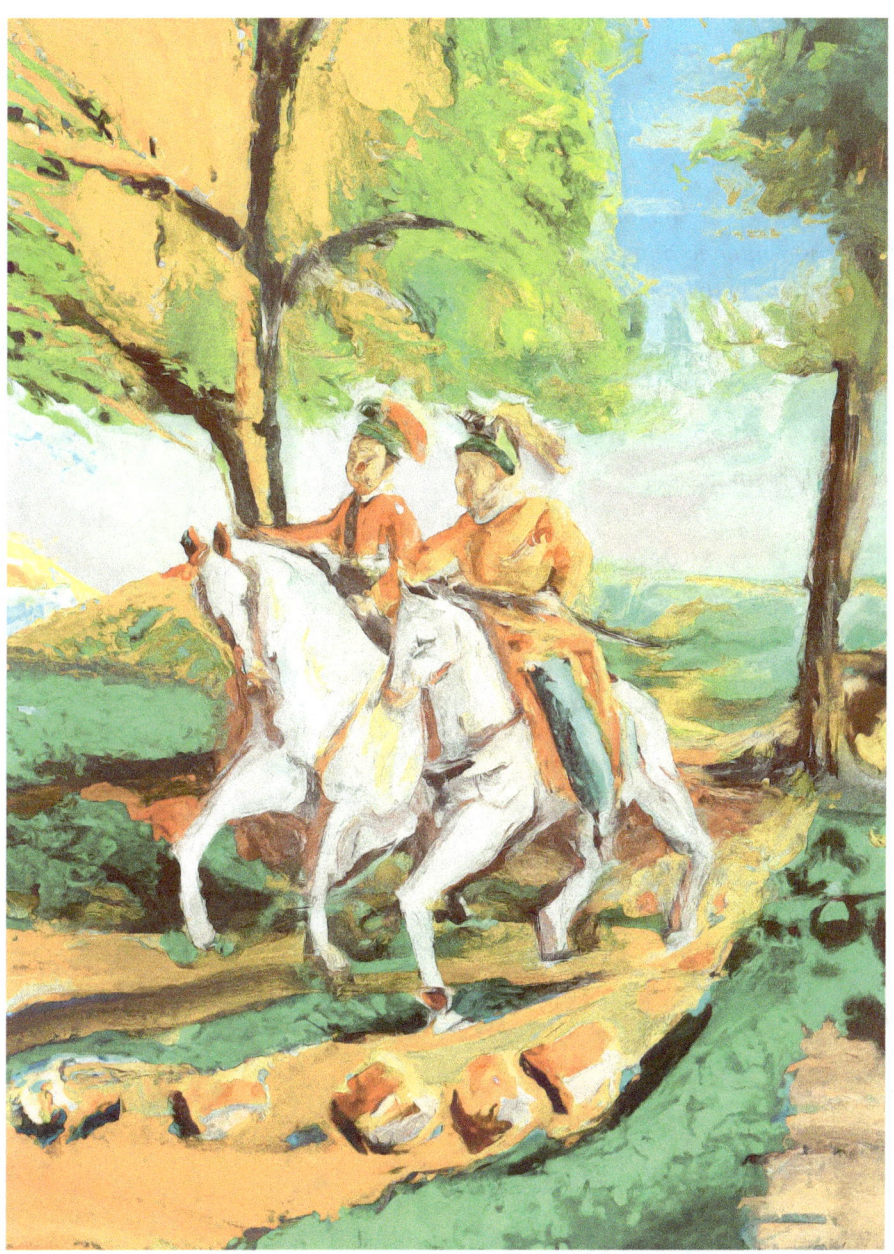

## Bucharest

*Flowered villas.*
*From the boat on the lake,*
*I see the whitened houses,*
*the gardens with orchards.*

*Calm, open people*
*stop, listen to you, explain.*
*The dry leaves smell,*
*burnt by tram rails.*

*Rain falls*
*on roasted, steaming chestnuts,*
*petroleum and bitumen*
*alternate in the air,*
*and in the distance, you hear the sawmill,*
*cutting wood.*

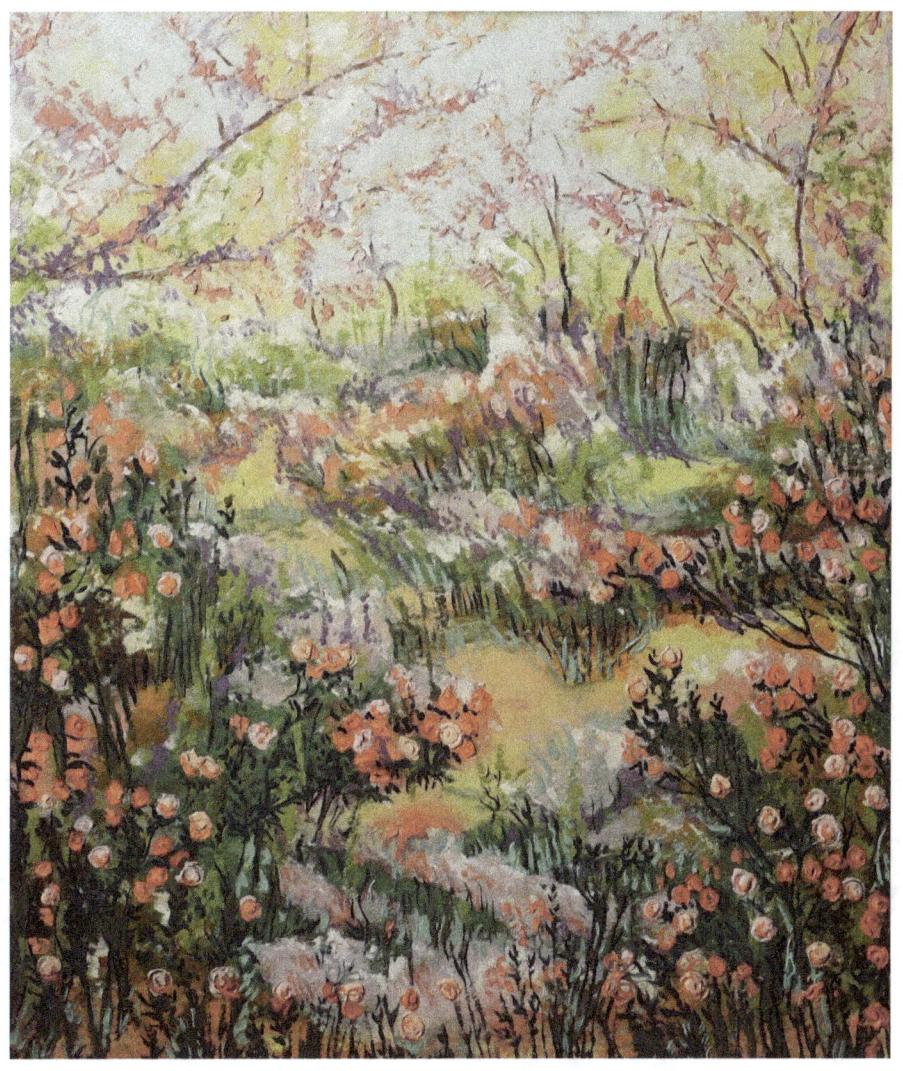

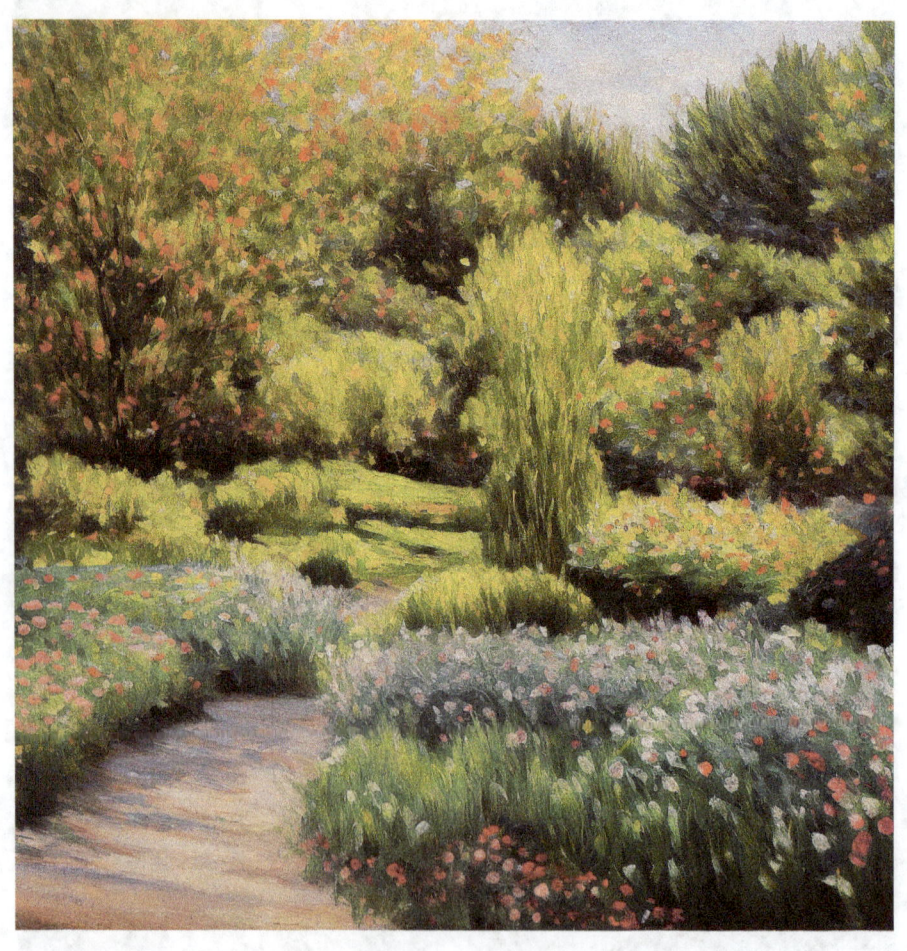

## Viper

*Always from the seed you sow,*
*sprouts with the shining of the sun*
*a straight path, not a lie,*
*so sow that which you sow.*

*Flee away from the evil bloodline,*
*bow with holy water,*
*wet your face and hands.*

*Out of habit or because it's evil,*
*it will want to spy on you and tell you about them,*
*for the bright sun gives its goodness.*

*Crawling and slimy serpent,*
*warming itself up, late it will want.*

## The nest

*A nest on the balcony.*
*A swallow spins desperate,*
*if I go out on the balcony.*

*Swallows run and gather*
*all around, and circles in flight*
*they make until my return.*

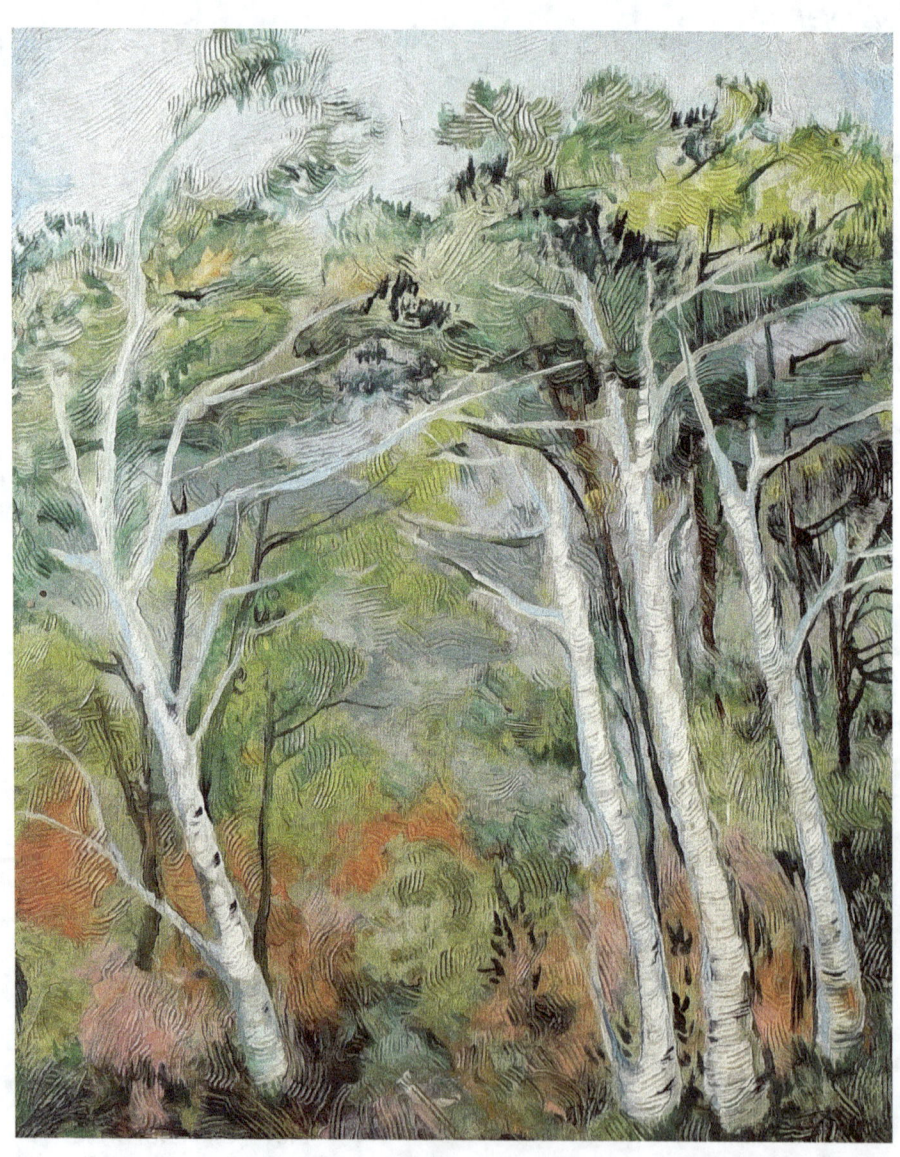

# As art hopes

*It has the same order*
*and the same greatness.*
*Like dying,*
*it's like losing,*
*like being afraid,*
*and it's like not remembering.*

*It's decaying from the sky,*
*erasing life.*
*Preserve it...*
*Hold it with all*
*its images,*
*its very existence.*

*And then the others, to the infinite...*
*And don't encounter*
*its non-hope,*
*which is true death.*

*The world is filled*
*with living deads.*
*Give back the memory to being*
*to its art gallery.*

# BIOGRAPHY

Maria Giacomello was born in Bucharest in 1935 to an Italian father, Mario Giacomello, and a Moldavian mother, Eufrasina Karpovnov Surucianov. She began her studies in painting at the age of 9, under the guidance of her father, later followed by masters such as A. G. Verona, I. D. Stefanescu, and G. Popescu. At the age of 12, with the assistance of Professor G. Popovici, she was admitted to the Tudor Academy in Bucharest, where she further improved her painting technique, studying alongside with the group of painters from the Nicolae Grigorescu Academic Institute of Fine Arts.

In 1951, she moved to Italy with her family, settling in Novara. Here, she became a part of the Cenacolo degli Artisti Piemontesi (Circle of Piedmontese Artists), headed by the sculptor Tantardini. For six years, she took part in the group's collective exhibitions and attended the Fine Arts Institute directed by Nino Di Salvatore, who taught her Italian art history and introduced her to modern art. From the collective exhibitions in 1952-53, she moved on to her first solo exhibitions at Broletto in Novara in 1954-55. During the triennium from 1957 to 1960, she was drawn to the regional art of Piedmont, particularly Novara, which influenced her to express herself through the personal style of "painting vorticism", enriched by that "material color" which will become one of her most remarkable features.

In 1961, she underwent the first tragedy of her life, the death of her father. She sunk into a deep crisis that compelled her to revisit the streets of her childhood in Romania, where she started to sign her works as Karpovnov Surucianov. During this period, she received awards and honors, and her poetry were recognized by the Romanian Academy and the Tiberian Academy of Rome. In 1962, she was awarded the Silver Medal for Journalism in Amalfi.

She moved to Buenos Aires, Argentina, for two years, where she got married and had her first child. In 1964, she returned to Italy, initially settling in Todi and later in Milan, where her second child was born. Here, Maria Giacomello promoted Romanian artists and, in 1967, established the Cultural Center of Foreign Artists, organizing collective exhibitions featuring Eastern European painters. It was during this new phase of her artistic effort that she began signing her works as Giacomello da Bucarest, in memory of her paternal name. From 1969 to 1972, she continued her intense activities at the Cultural Center, promoting exhibitions, encouraging journals reviews, and engaging in social initiatives by donating artworks to various organizations and institutions.

In the years 1974 and 1975, she received prestigious recognitions: the Platinum Medal at the ASLA Prize, awarded by the Presidency of the Council of Ministers, recognizing her as a distinguished artist in culture; the Golden Plaque at the Expo Arte Internazionale in Milan; the Silver Ambrogino (Milan 1976) for her contributions to the Orthodox Community of the city. Other certificates and honors followed, such as the Palma d'Oro Trophy from the Guglielmo Marconi Academy in Rome, the Lauro d'Oro, and the Targa d'Oro Amici del Quadrato, received in Milan. During this particularly productive period, the artist combined sculpture with her painting, for which she received the Vittoria Alata Trophy at the Biennale d'Arte in La Spezia. In 1985, the Inter-American Academy of Human Sciences in Buenos Aires awarded her an Honorary Doctorate in Art.

In 1988, Maria Giacomello's life was overturned by a new sorrow, the loss of her second child, which led to an emotional blackout that blocked her creativity and dedication for eight years, until 1994 when she resumed painting as Karpov, thus reclaiming her own primal artistic name. In these later years, her painting became more melancholic and discreet, without the drive to participate in exhibitions and artistic awards. The initial enthusiasm gave way to a delicate awareness that time, with its changes, could be put at the service of her artistic sensitivity in a more complete and meaningful way. Evidence of this is that her relentless search for new figurative solutions ultimately settled into her latest painting style, as to confirm her achieved and hard-earned artistic maturity.

# AWARDS

1959 First Prize "Quinta Edizione Rassegna Pittura San Rocco" – Novara

1960 First Prize "Arte in Vetrina" - Novara

1961 First Prize "Mimosa d'Oro" – Novara

1961 First Prize E. Mattei E.N.I. – Novara

1962 ENI and Santa Barbara Award - Milan

1963 Silver Medal for Journalism – Amalfi

1965 Recognition of Merit with Gold Medal – Amalfi 65 – Rome

1966 Award for Extemporaneous Pro Loco Santhia – Milan

1967 Third Place with Prize in the National Art Competition of Varesina – Varese

1968 Appointed Member of the Permanente di Milano - Milan

1968 Diploma of Merit with Gold Medal in the National Competition ANRP "Bagliori d'Eroismo" – Milan

1971 Diploma of Merit "10 Years of Italian Poetry" International Academy of Cultural Propaganda - Rome

1972 Diploma of Merit "Painters for Maladjusted Children" Lions Milano Host – Milan

1972 Appointment with Gold Medal as "Academic of Tiberina" - Rome

1975 Gold Plaque for Expo Arte Internazionale - Milan

1975 Decennial Prize "Distinguished in Culture" ASLA – Palermo

1975 Recognition Prize with Gold Medal – Cultural and Artistic Contacts –

Pompeii

1976 Appointment as Honorary Academic of the Universal Academy of Sciences, Culture, and Arts – Rome

1976 Ambrogino Medal at the Orthodox Church Crypt Conference - Milan

1978 Appointment as Honorary Academic with Gold Medal Academy Italy-Salsomaggiore Terme

1979 Silver Ambrogino Prize for the Romanian Orthodox Community - Milan

1979 Gold Plaque "Pall Sormai" - Grand Prize Association Amici del Quadrato – Milan

1979 Prize at the 6th International Prize "Natale d'oro" Art Mondial – Milan

1983 Presentation of the Prize with the Statue Vittoria Alata – World Culture Prize – Milan

1984 Gold Plaque of the Art Biennale Critics – La Spezia

1985 Honorary Diploma as an Art Expert – Intercontinental Institute of Modern Art – Brescia

1986 Honorary Degree "Doctor of Art" – Center for Studies and Research of Nations – Cremona

1986 "Palma d'Oro Europa" Award – European Academy Italy

1986 Honorary Degree from Universidad Interamericana de Ciensas Umanisticas – Buenos Ayres

1987 First Prize Lauro d'Oro and Appointment as Artistic Advisor – Academy Italy – Rome

1988 Diploma of Academic Master – Academy of Masters

1989 First Prize "Trofeo Bacchiglione" – Cultural Artistic Center "Proposte d'Arte" – Milan

1990 Hax 1990 Award – Direction of the Institute of Contemporary Art – Milan

1996 International Abstract Art Painting Prize – Carrara Hallstahammar – Carrara

2001 First Prize Painting Competition "La Chiesa dell'Incoronata" Artists Association Garibaldi – Milan

2002 S'Ambrogio d'Oro Artistic Award – Association Amici del Quadrato – Milan

2006 Appointment as Art Expert by the Alternative Academy and National

Federation of Art Experts – Milan
2006 Art Recognition Prize "Gran Trofeo Michelangelo" - Quadrato - Milan